HOW TO BUY REAL ESTATE OVERSEAS

HOW TO BUY REAL ESTATE OVERSEAS

KATHLEEN PEDDICORD

WILEY

For general information about our other products and services, please contact our Customer Care Department within the United States at (800) 762-2974, outside the United States at (317) 572-3993 or fax (317) 572-4002.

Wiley publishes in a variety of print and electronic formats and by print-on-demand. Some material included with standard print versions of this book may not be included in e-books or in print-on-demand. If this book refers to media such as a CD or DVD that is not included in the version you purchased, you may download this material at http://booksupport.wiley.com. For more information about Wiley products, visit www.wiley.com.

Library of Congress Cataloging-in-Publication Data:

Peddicord, Kathleen.

  How to buy real estate overseas / Kathleen Peddicord.
      pages cm
    Includes index.
    ISBN 978-1-118-51859-5 (cloth); ISBN 978-1-118-60741-1 (ebk);
    ISBN 978-1-118-60742-8 (ebk); ISBN 978-1-118-60753-4 (ebk)
  1. Real estate investment—Foreign countries. 2. Retirement, Places of—Foreign countries. 3. Retirees—Life skills guides. 4. Americans—Foreign countries. I. Title.
    HD1382.5.P43 2013
    332.63'24—dc23
                                                                2012047944

For Bill and Mark, who got me started.

Contents

Launching Your Overseas Property Adventure

I 've told the buyer from Dublin that the other buyer, the gentleman from Cork, is considering by how much he'd be willing to increase his offer," John Rohan explained in a hurry as he burst through the door into the little room where my husband, Lief, and I sat waiting. "However, the other buyer, the one from Cork, he's gone. He said he'd reached his limit and excused himself from the bidding. He's left the building. Our buyer from Dublin doesn't know this, but it won't be long before he figures it out. This is your chance. If you're selling, you're selling today, now. I believe I can push the Dublin bidder up another 50,000 euro, but that's all I'm going to get out of him."

With that, Mr. Rohan looked squarely at Lief and then at me, gauging our reactions. I glanced over at the monitor mounted on the wall to our right. The room where we'd been told to wait while John Rohan presided over the auction for our home in Waterford, Ireland, had no windows. The monitor on the wall was our only glimpse of the activity going on around us. It showed the auction room itself, where we'd watched, starting an hour earlier, as Mr. Rohan had opened bidding for our Lahardan House before a crowd of about three dozen people. John had prepared us by explaining that most in the room would be bystanders, there just to see what the house might sell for. In the end, we had five serious bidders. Three pulled out quickly, leaving the gentleman from Cork and the gentleman from Dublin, who'd been going back and forth, first in the main auction room and then, eventually, from two separate, private rooms where John Rohan had escorted each in turn, for more than 30 minutes.

The year was 2004, and the Celtic Tiger was roaring. All Ireland was watching all the time to see by how much more property values had appreciated since the last time they'd checked. We'd purchased our Lahardan House, the property on the block that day, about six years earlier. John Rohan's projected selling price, more than $900,000 at the euro-dollar exchange rate of the day, had us tripling our investment. Why were we hesitating to accept it?

Because overseas property investing isn't only about the money.

I've hosted conferences on living, retiring, and investing in real estate overseas for more than 25 years. Lately I've taken to asking the crowd at each of these events a series of questions.

First: "How many of you are thinking about buying property overseas for investment?" A few hands shoot up.

Then: "How many of you are considering purchasing a retirement residence in another country?" A flurry of hands in the air.

Finally: "How many of you would like what I'd term a 'second home overseas,' a place you intend to occupy, full- or part-time, in retirement or sooner, if possible, but that you hope could earn some income when you're not using it yourself?" At the suggestion of this, practically every person in the room raises his or her hand.

These folks seem to understand something that it's taken Lief and me more than 15 years of marriage and more than three dozen property purchases in 21 countries to figure out. Buying real estate overseas makes so much more sense when you do it as part of a big-picture plan.

I didn't set out to become an overseas property investor. It happened by accident and organically. When my husband of but three months, my eight-year-old daughter, and I arrived in Waterford, Ireland, 15 years ago, we needed a place to live. I like old houses the way some women like new shoes and was drawn to the idea of owning an Irish Georgian-style house in the country, a place surrounded by rolling green fields dotted with roaming sheep and spotted cows and bordered by low stone walls and tidy hedge-rows. My new husband didn't object, and after a search that extended nearly a year, we purchased Lahardan House, a 200-year-old stone house on 6 acres that became our first home as a new family.

Lahardan House was where my daughter, Kaitlin, born and raised to this point in Baltimore, Maryland, struggled with the transition to our new life overseas and where we welcomed our son, Jackson, born in Waterford just two months after we'd moved in. It was where Kaitlin learned to ride a pony in the front pasture and where Jackson learned to walk in the forever muddy back garden. Lahardan House was our first overseas renovation adventure. The old stone house was dripping with damp, its timbers riddled with rot when we bought it. In time, we transformed it into a comfortable and cozy home kept warm and dry by the big Stanley stove in the kitchen.

Lahardan House was also our first overseas property success story, and not only because, in the end, we accepted the offer that John Rohan coaxed from the gentleman bidder from Dublin, putting aside our emotional attachment to the place and tripling our money. More important, our experience with Lahardan House taught us the fundamentals related to buying and selling real estate overseas that we've learned to respect most, key among which is this: The best purchases are made with your calculator, yes, but also with your heart.

When Lief and I went looking for a house to buy in Ireland years ago, I was shopping for rolling green hills, centuries-old stone walls, tumble-down outbuildings, and classic Georgian symmetry. He was shopping for cost per square meter, rate of appreciation, and projected return on investment (ROI). Today, dozens of often conflicted purchases later, we finally understand that the secret to success in buying and selling real estate overseas is recognizing that each of these seemingly competing perspectives is important and that each deserves equal weight in any buy decision.

After we sold Lahardan House, we took those proceeds, added about 20 percent to them, and reinvested in an apartment in Paris. For our money, we got less than one-quarter the space we'd enjoyed in Ireland. Not a sensible exchange of values, you might say, at least not if you're evaluating the transaction using your calculator alone.

We were moving to Paris so that our daughter could attend her final three years of high school in France and so that our little family could, meantime, sample life in the City of Light, a dream of mine since I was a young girl. Certainly, under those circumstances, we could have rented a place to live. We didn't need to buy an apartment for our time in Paris, and as I said, on the face of it, going by the numbers alone, buying an apartment in Paris didn't add up. Yet that's what we did.

Now, in retrospect, I can say that the apartment we purchased in Paris's seventh *arrondissement* has proved, like Lahardan House in Ireland, to be one of the most successful investment decisions of our careers, again, we understand now, because it wasn't made for investment reasons alone. We own this Paris apartment still, return to visit it as often as we're able, and rent it out when we're not using it ourselves. It has evolved into one of our most valued assets, in part because it's worth about twice what we paid for it, but also, more important to us, because it has become the cornerstone of our retirement. We didn't purchase this apartment as an eventual retirement residence. However, the more time we spent living in Paris, the more we liked living in Paris. Finally, Lief and I agreed that we'd always like living in Paris, that this is a place we'll always want a chance and an excuse to return to. The apartment we bought to live in while our daughter finished her high school education and that we've held on to for occasional use and cash flow from rental income ever since, thereby was transformed, organically, into a piece of our long-term retirement plan.

Ann and Mike's Caribbean Adventure

When you approach the idea of buying real estate overseas in this way, organically and in stages, it can be much easier to organize your dream life, whatever that is, than you might imagine. Take my friend Ann, for example. In February 1999, Ann and her husband, Mike, traveled to San Pedro, Ambergris Caye, Belize, for the first time. They were on an adventure tour.

As Ann explains it today, "We had no idea what momentous life changes would occur as a result of that fateful trip. We simply wanted to escape to our own little piece of heaven. For us, that meant a Caribbean island. I couldn't wait to get back into scuba diving, and I knew that Belize's stunning Barrier Reef would be an ideal choice for this. We did have it in our minds that if we liked Belize as much as we thought we would based on our research, we might buy a place of our own there. An investment near the Caribbean Sea seemed like a no-brainer in 1999."

Ann and Mike traveled the entire country of Belize, and, at the end of the weeklong tour, Ann explains, "Our hearts led us back to Ambergris Caye." The couple was so taken with the little island that they made a deposit on a piece of property at the end of that first trip. "Our intention," Ann remembers, "was to vacation in Belize. We weren't even thinking about retirement. Not yet 50, I'd just stepped into a lucrative VP position for a Fortune 500 company. Life was good. We just wanted a place to escape for regular doses of Caribbean sun and sea."

Ann's husband, Mike, is an architect. Mike spent the year after he and Ann made their initial Belize island purchase designing and erecting a small condo building. The couple sold the bottom two apartments and lived in the top one. Mike was on the island much of the time, focused on his construction project, but Ann was traveling back and forth between Ambergris and California.

"In the process of coming and going on vacation that first year," Ann explains, "something unexpected happened. I got hooked on the community's spirit. I quickly felt at home in this quirky, charming little town. Even people I'd met only once remembered my name. Everyone waved and welcomed me back each time they saw me. This was a small-town environment I'd never experienced. The sense of community was irresistible for me."

Over the next few years, Ann and Mike developed a plan to live in Belize part-time. Mike decided to sell the condo project he'd completed and next bought 6 acres on which the couple planned to develop the island's first fitness club. They built and then operated the San Pedro Fitness Center for five years. "Those were exceptionally fun times for us," Ann says.

In 2008, the couple made two more big decisions. One was to sell the club to a development company. The other was to move to the island full-time.

"Finally," Ann says, "I was ready to take early retirement and walk away from my corporate position. I had worked as a manager in the environmental field for more than 30 years. That was enough. Plus, I could see changes coming in the United States, changes that led me to worry about Mike's and my future. It was time to make a move, while we were still young enough to build new lives for ourselves."

The cost of living in Belize is considerably lower than in most of the United States, including in San Francisco. That was an important determining factor for Ann and Mike. Another was the chance for adventure. That's what had attracted them to Belize in the first place. Finally, they felt they had the confidence to pursue that agenda full-time.

How has all this worked out for Ann and Mike? "Do we still love this country and this island?" Ann wonders. "You bet! Let's face it. No country is perfect. But our lives have been incredibly rich and diverse since we made this move. Much of our satisfaction flows from the charm, beauty, and comfort of this unique country and our quirky little island. We continue to appreciate the good nature of the Belizean people, their commitment to a free and democratic society, and their intense community spirit. English as a first language made our transition easy. And the solid banking and legal systems give us comfort. The Internet, phone, and utility services are reliable on Ambergris Caye. We have access to most of the amenities we had in the United States, but that's not what keeps us so happy here.

"We've been able to re-create our lives through challenging but satisfying transitions. From building our own homes to starting, operating, and selling new businesses, each transition has been an adventure and life-changing. We would not have had these options or opportunities in the San Francisco Bay region, and each step has been one of self-discovery. I am grateful that fate brought us to this unique country and that we had the opportunity to take the transition one step at a time. That worked for us. We've had some major successes, and we've had some major disappointments, but I wouldn't trade this experience for anything."

1

This Isn't Only about Making Money

What Is Your Dream?

That's the place to start. What lifestyle are you looking for, and what other objectives are you hoping to achieve? In short, why are you thinking about buying real estate overseas?

Here are potential reasons why you are smart to be considering this idea right now:

Reason 1. Like real estate anywhere, real estate overseas is a hard asset, and, in the current investment climate, hard assets are the most sensible investment class, the best choice for storing value.

Reason 2. As with real estate anywhere, you're buying with the hope of capital appreciation, but you can also be buying for cash flow, currently an important investment agenda item.

Reason 3. Real estate overseas provides portfolio diversification—diversification of currency, diversification of market, and diversification of asset type (rental, raw land, condo-hotel, etc.).

Reason 4. Real estate overseas provides the opportunity for you to position yourself to profit from both expanding and crisis markets.

Reason 5. Real estate overseas can double as a retirement plan—today's investment can be tomorrow's retirement residence.

Reason 6. Real estate overseas can double as a holiday home, an investment that you and your family are able to use and enjoy from the day you make it.

Reason 7. Real estate overseas can be part of a legacy of wealth that you leave to your heirs.

Reason 8. Real estate overseas is safe and private, one of but two remaining asset types that an American need not report to the IRS every year.

Reason 9. A real estate investment overseas can bring tax advantages, including deductions you can take on your U.S. tax return.

Reviewing this list of reasons to buy real estate overseas, you notice that the big picture breaks down into two categories—category 1: investment, and category 2: lifestyle. These different agendas, as I've been describing, should be considered in unison for the best results.

Another thing to notice about this list of reasons to put your time and money into the acquisition of real estate overseas is that, fundamentally, it's all about diversification. That is the real advantage of this strategy—diversification of your portfolio and your assets, but diversification, too, of your life, your retirement, and your legacy.

We are living at a time that presents the opportunity to take the investor's profit agenda, combine it with the live-better-for-less agenda of the retiree, and transfer it overseas. It is an opportunity to use overseas real estate as both an investment vehicle and a strategy for a new and better life, both immediately and longer term in retirement. Overseas real estate amounts to the surest strategy for creating and preserving legacy wealth while simultaneously reinventing your life and rescuing your retirement. Thanks to global market events of the past half-dozen years, many options exist right now for where to buy to make money while also making a new life, and, thanks to the Internet, it is possible today to seize these opportunities easily and cost-effectively to build a new life while staying in touch in real time with family, friends, business concerns, and investment portfolios from the old one.

The best case is when you are able to find a piece of real estate in a place where you want to spend time, short term on vacation and long term in retirement, that also holds out the potential for an investment return, in the form of capital appreciation, rental return, or both. This perfect storm of objectives should be your ultimate goal. A holiday home on the beach of Nicaragua can become little more than a headache and a carrying cost if you ultimately decide you can't abide life in the tropics.

Could You Really Do This?

The reasons to diversify your investment portfolio and your lifestyle to include real estate overseas have never been more compelling than they are right now. But you may be thinking, who does this, really? Isn't this a strategy of the jet set? No, it's not.

I come from middle-class Baltimore; Lief, from middle-class Phoenix. We started our overseas real estate adventures with next to nothing. (Lief made his first property investment using a $5,000 gift from a family member. I'll tell you more about this later.) I've been covering the live-and-invest-overseas beat for nearly three decades. In that time, I've met thousands of others, at conferences and in my travels, who, likewise, have built adventure-filled lives that include real estate holdings overseas, and I can't think of one of them who I'd describe as jet set. These are all regular folks.

They represent all demographics. A friend, Lee, took early retirement at the age of 49 from a successful engineering career based in Manhattan and moved first to Ecuador, then to Uruguay, next to Brazil, and, most recently, last year, to Colombia. In each case, Lee bought a home, and, in each case, he was rewarded. A significant part of Lee's income over the past 12 years of his retirement has come from his serial home ownership in each of the countries where he's been retired.

"I didn't have enough of a pension or enough retirement savings to live on for the rest of my life in the States, certainly not living the level of lifestyle my wife and I had been enjoying in New York up until that point," Lee explains. "So I started looking around for options. My eyes were opened to the 'retire overseas' option by a book on retiring to Costa Rica that I happened upon in a bookstore one day. At that point in our lives, my wife, Julie, and I wanted a big change, an adventure. We craved culture shock, the bigger the better. So while Costa Rica was the first country I considered as an overseas option, it wasn't the one we chose for the start of our overseas adventures. Julie and I chose Ecuador, where we embraced a very different and almost unbelievably affordable lifestyle.

"We enjoyed Ecuador, but, once we'd made that first move, we couldn't help but notice other options that also seemed very appealing. What could be better than Ecuador, we'd asked ourselves while enjoying our new life there, first in Cuenca, then in Vilcabamba. Then we discovered that, well, other places might just be better in some ways. So, from Ecuador, we moved to Uruguay, where we divided our time between Montevideo and Punta del

Este, on the coast. What could be better than that life, split between a pleasant city and one of the world's most beautiful stretches of coastline?

"Then we discovered Brazil, where we lived right on the beach. Could we top that? In fact, we believe we have now, in Medellín. Given the quality of lifestyle and the quality of property that you're buying, this place is an extraordinary bargain."

Another friend, Coley, made his first overseas real estate purchase at the age of 35. Coley and his wife, Allison, weren't worried about money, making ends meet, or how they'd pay for retirement. Coley was making a great living, the young couple and their two small children were enjoying a fully appointed life in Washington, D.C., and retirement was decades away. Looking ahead, their lives seemed to promise lots more of the same—more earnings and an even more comfortable lifestyle as they continued to work hard and make their way up the D.C. ladder. They had achieved, at early ages, the life that many Americans dream about.

Only it wasn't working for them. From their position in the U.S. capital, they had an insider's view of what was going on and, from their perspective, what was going wrong. This was seven years ago, and, after a lot of research and months of soul-searching, Coley and his wife, in their mid-30s, scooped up their two little ones and opted out. "We wanted to get out while we were still young enough to remake our lives and our children's futures in a way that made more sense to us."

Coley and his young family hopped a flight from the American capital to the Panamanian one, where, months before, they'd purchased a house on the beach. They had to pull the trigger on their plan, because their house back in the States had sold. Yet, they discovered, their new home on the coast outside Panama City wasn't finished yet. Arriving in Panama, the little family checked into the Intercontinental Hotel.

"We were at the Intercontinental for weeks," Coley explains. "I would wake up in the middle of the night in a cold sweat. What was I doing? We were living in a hotel in a Third World city with two toddlers, for crying out loud. Burning through our savings. No one could promise when our house would be ready for us to move in. I thought I'd made the biggest mistake of my life."

Today, seven years later, Coley is confident that moving his family to Panama was the smartest thing he could have done at the time and that, if he hadn't done it then, he'd do it today for sure. "I look at what's going on back in the States," he says, "and I know we made the right choice. I see very bad times ahead for my country. I think my family and I can do better for ourselves in this life we're creating for ourselves."

In the seven years since they took their leap of faith, Coley and his wife have welcomed a new member into their family (their third child was born in Panama City about a year ago), they've started businesses, including a school in the area where they're living because no international school existed anywhere nearby and, as Coley explains, "We got tired of homeschooling the kids," and now they're preparing to launch a sustainable community, to create a place where like-minded folks can work together to build the lives and futures they want.

"I'm back in the States regularly," Coley explains. "I travel to D.C. every month to work with my consulting clients. When we meet, all they want to talk about is my life here in Panama. 'What's Panama really like?' . . . 'Do you have any regrets?' they want to know. 'Man, I wish I could do it,' they say. 'Boy, Coley, you've figured this out. Do you think I could do it, too?'

"There's so much unhappiness and uncertainty in the United States right now, especially in D.C. I think people in that part of the country are at the epicenter of a growing recognition that things are out of control. What I realized years ago was that nobody was going to get things back under control anytime soon. Our only choice, each of us, is to take control of our own lives. I say this to friends and clients back in D.C. today, and they agree. They see this truth as well as I do. But they're scared, intimidated. I understand. I was scared, too, when the realization first set in for me."

The idea of diversifying your investments, your assets, your life, and your future overseas can seem frightening, intimidating, even paralyzing. Could you really do it? Yes, you could. I say that based on 30 years of experience at this. Ann and Mike, Lee and Julie, Coley and Allison, Lief and me, we're all just regular folks, like you. If we could do it, so can you. How? Keep reading.

Can You Afford to Buy Real Estate Overseas?

The two most common reasons for resistance to the idea of investing in real estate overseas can be a general uncertainty about how to go about it and a more specific concern about the cost. Can the average investor or retiree really afford to pursue this strategy? Yes. You could get started with as little as $50,000 to $100,000 of working capital, sometimes less.

The most sensible first purchase is a small place (house or apartment) in a country where you want to spend time and where you have a reasonable expectation of generating some cash flow from rental. Given a budget of $50,000 to $100,000, you could purchase a piece of property that you could use part-time and rent out otherwise in Abruzzo, Italy; Béarn, France; Cork, Ireland; Cuenca, Ecuador; Medellín, Colombia; Granada, Nicaragua; or Cayo, Belize, to name a handful of examples. You wouldn't be buying big or fancy, but small and modest is the way to start anyway. Big and fancy means heavy carrying costs. Property taxes usually depend on the size of the property. A big house on a big lot needs lots of cleaning, landscaping, and caretaking. And a fancy house is one you're more likely to worry about being damaged by renters. Starting out, especially if your budget is limited, you want one or two bedrooms and standard finishes, fixtures, and furnishings. This is not to say you don't want charming. In Abruzzo and Béarn, to stick with my two examples in the Old World, even $50,000 to $100,000 can buy you a lot of charm.

Most property markets outside the United States are cash-only. I'll address this important topic in full later. Note now that, while all cash at closing is the standard in most of the world, you can arrange bank financing as a foreign buyer in Panama (though it's not always easy) and most of Europe (where it can be a very straightforward process), and in most developing markets you can pursue developer or seller financing. Given the current credit climate in the United States, it's all but impossible for an American to borrow back home (via home equity) for the purchase of real estate overseas. Developers in markets that cater to American buyers understand this and are more open today to selling on time than they've ever been. As I write, I know of three developers in three different "developing" markets (Belize, Nicaragua, and Panama) who are offering very appealing terms. In each case, you could buy with $30,000 down or less and payments of as little as $1,000 per month.

Ecuador, Colombia, Nicaragua, Belize, and Panama, therefore, qualify as good starter markets, places where you can buy with less than $100,000 and where seller/developer financing is possible. With $100,000 to $200,000 to spend, your options expand to include Uruguay, France, Italy, Spain, and Croatia. You might even find something in that range in Ireland. With $200,000 to $300,000, you could buy almost anywhere.

How Can You Be Sure Something Won't Go Wrong?

You can't. It will. There are risks, and, as with any kind of investing, nothing is guaranteed. Don't let that deter you. What's the option? To do nothing? To keep your assets, your retirement, and your future all at home, all in one place? Would that be safer or more prudent? No.

You must diversify both your investments and your life. It's a necessity of the world we're living in. Don't worry. I'll walk you through it.

2

Buy Overseas to Diversify Your Assets, Protect Your Wealth, and Avoid Taxes while Creating Cash Flow and Profits

In April 2000, my husband, Lief, drove the southern coast of Spain from France to Portugal while scouting real estate investment opportunities. This was in the early days of focused development along the Spanish *costa,* before property markets in this part of the world bubbled up and boiled over. It was a time when it was possible to buy preconstruction (off-plan, as it's referred to by European developers) for little down and then sell on the contract before having to close on the purchase, walking away with impressive returns for not much capital out of pocket. Lief met with a developer who had just launched a new project on the beach in Estepona. The terms were typical of the times, with a down payment of 5 percent and further 5 percent deposits at key points throughout the period of construction until reaching 30 percent. The balance would be due when the unit was completed and delivered. Lief sized up the market and the developer and signed a contract.

At the time, foreigners could get easy financing in Spain for up to 70 percent loan to value, meaning we had a security net for coming up with the balance due beyond the preconstruction payments. However, the exit strategy was to flip the unit before completion (as is the goal with most preconstruction investments). Construction was scheduled to take 24 months. After signing the contract and making the initial 5 percent down payment, we listed the unit with the developer for resale almost immediately. As we bought into the first units of the first building in what was planned as a three-building complex, our unit was among the first built and therefore the most sought after as the developer neared completion. Most end users wanted to be able to move in immediately.

A few months before having to make the decision as to whether to get a mortgage to close or to use other available investment funds, the developer wrote to say he had a buyer. The transaction was put together so that that buyer acquired our contract, paying us our 30 percent deposit plus our profit (the difference between the preconstruction price and what we sold for). Then the buyer paid the developer 70 percent of the original price at closing. Clean and clear-cut.

It was a model preconstruction investment. We walked away with an annualized return of 30 percent per year over two and a half years.

In 2004, we made another preconstruction purchase, this one in Panama City. As in Spain, this was before prices started taking off in this market, and, as in Spain, we bought from a developer with long experience and a solid track record. That's critical when buying preconstruction. It's no guarantee that you won't lose money or that the developer will be able to deliver what you're expecting, but it does reduce those risks. The location for the unit we bought in Panama City was prime, front-line to the ocean in the center of the city, an address we believed would hold value long term as the Panamanian capital continued to develop.

Our exit strategy for this purchase was different than for the purchase in Spain. We didn't buy for quick capital appreciation with the intention of selling on the contract before closing on the purchase. Rather, we bought to take a position in the rental market expansion that we perceived in this city. High-quality, well-located, one-bedroom units hadn't existed in Panama's capital up to that point. Meantime, the numbers of retirees, businesspeople, and tourists moving through the city in search of rentals fitting that description were increasing quickly.

By the time our unit was completed (at the beginning of 2007), the market had appreciated significantly, and the global real estate crash was still a year in the future. Some investors flipped out of their units as they were delivered and realized gains of as much as 100 percent over their purchase prices. A year later, prices came down, but they never dropped as low as the original preconstruction prices.

People who didn't flip their unit and who hadn't bought for personal use put their apartment up for rental. This included Lief and me. In 2007 and 2008, we saw short-term rental yields of 12 percent net per year. We'd chosen to rent furnished (believing this would bring greater return long term), and our double-digit net yield reflected not only the total purchase price but also the cost of furnishing. At the end of 2008, the short-term rental market in Panama City hit a wall, but the long-term market remained strong, so we decided to transition our apartment from a short- to a long-term rental. Our net annual yield was reduced but has continued steady and stable ever since at about 8 percent per year. The same tenant remains in the unit as I write. In addition, if we sold today, we'd be looking at about a 35 percent gain on the preconstruction price we paid.

These are two examples of how to buy real estate overseas for investment and investment alone. Lief and I had no intention of holding onto the preconstruction condo we purchased on the coast of Spain because we don't like that part of that country's coast (it's overdeveloped). We intended to keep the Panama City apartment but as a rental investment property, not as a place to use ourselves (it's too small for our family). In both cases, we broke our rule about marrying the investor's agenda with a lifestyle one. We've broken this rule other times in the past and likely will again. My point is that you can approach overseas real estate as an investment, period. You can eliminate any element of personal use and still decide to buy to a good end.

Real Estate Is a Real Asset

You understand already, I'm sure, the fundamental reasons why real estate is attractive as an investment class. A piece of real estate anywhere in the world is a real asset that you control and that, barring some act of God, can't disappear altogether. (I knew a guy years ago whose beachfront lot on the shore of Montserrat was destroyed in a volcano eruption, but that kind of thing is rare.) Furthermore, buy right, and your property investment can grow in value and deliver reliable cash flow. Certainly, if you've bought right, with an eye to intrinsic value, your asset should hold its value. It can also be productive, growing things—teak trees, for example—that provide additional value on their own. Plus, real estate is an asset you can use. Depending on what you buy, you could vacation in it, retire in it, or lend it out to your children and your friends. All things considered, as investors have understood for centuries, real estate is one of the soundest investment strategies you can pursue.

The current opportunity, though, is bigger. In the present global financial climate, not real estate in general, but real estate overseas, specifically, is the smartest thing you can do with your capital, be it earmarked for investment or retirement.

The Ultimate Diversification Strategy

First, real estate overseas is the ultimate diversification strategy at a time when diversification beyond U.S. markets and outside the U.S. dollar is more important than ever before in our history and certainly more important than ever before in our lifetimes. No matter how many kinds of investments you hold, if they're all U.S.-based or all U.S. dollar–denominated, you are not diversified. You are at the mercy of U.S. markets and events, and that's a dangerous place to be right now.

The Current Cycle of Crisis

Second, the current global climate of crisis that is creating the urgent need for the investor to diversify across asset types, across markets, and across currencies, is creating opportunity as well. U.S. property markets aren't the only ones collapsing. Real estate values in Ireland, Spain, and Nicaragua, to name three dramatic examples, are, too. Other markets, including Argentina, are moving toward collapse. Crisis creates opportunity, and, right now, the crisis opportunities are many and global.

Not All Markets Are Collapsing

On the other hand, the investor in search of global diversification (this should include all investors right now) would do well to remember that not all world markets are struggling or in recession. Certain places today present opportunity, especially for the investor in search of a yield (in the form of cash flow from rental income), thanks to expanding end-user markets— expanding local middle classes, for example, or growing numbers of international executives, foreign investors, global entrepreneurs, or expat retirees taking up residence. It's not only savvy property investors who are taking their agenda global. Entrepreneurs, investors of all kinds, and retirees as well are moving their capital, basing their activities, and relaunching their lives in places where they have reason to believe they'll be well treated. These migrating moneymakers bolster economies and expand markets wherever they settle.

No One Needs to Know (Not Even the IRS)

Another, more practical reason why real estate overseas is the smartest thing to do with your money right now has to do with privacy. As an American, no matter where you live (that is, whether you're resident in the United States or not), you are required to report all foreign financial assets to Uncle Sam each year on what is referred to as Form 8938 if you meet the reporting criteria. However, there are two exceptions to the 8938 filing requirement, that is, two foreign assets that the IRS doesn't insist on knowing about. One is gold and other precious metals (held in physical form). The other is real estate if it is held in your personal name (i.e., not held in a foreign corporation or foreign LLC). This means that foreign real estate is one of only two remaining assets that allow the American to retain some level of privacy of ownership, not only vis-à-vis Uncle Sam but also potential U.S. plaintiffs or creditors. How is a U.S. plaintiff going to seize your condo in Panama City or your beachfront lot in Belize? He's not.

Potentially Tax Deductible, Too

Another practical benefit for an American owning real estate outside the United States has to do with his annual tax bill. The travel associated with scouting for, purchasing, and then managing (in the case of a rental) a real estate investment overseas is tax deductible.

Years ago, I knew a woman named Janet who bought land on the southwestern coast of Ireland, in Kerry. On this land Janet built two houses, one for her personal use and one to rent out. Each summer, Janet took a trip to Kerry to check on her rental property and to meet with her rental manager. During the visit, she stayed in one of the two houses she'd built, her Irish home. The income from renting out the second of the two houses covered the carrying costs and then some for both properties, with money left over to subsidize Janet's annual holidays on the Emerald Isle. Then, every April 15, Janet was able to take those travel costs as deductions on her U.S. tax return.

How to Buy for Investment

Here's the thinking that should go into any overseas real estate purchase you consider for investment:

- **Economic Outlook.** Markets move up and down, and then up again. At what point in this cycle is the market where you're thinking about buying right now? In which direction is it moving and why? If the market is moving up quickly because of foreign buyers (think the Spanish *costas* up until 2008), can you expect that foreign interest to continue? If not, who else might your eventual buyer be? Also, is there a reasonable expectation for appreciation in property values? If so, in what timeframe—short, medium, or long term?

- **Inventory Supply and Demand.** In expanding markets, supply typically takes time to catch up with demand, helping to create peaks and valleys in pricing even if the overall trend is up. In Panama City, right now, for example, a glut of high-rise condos is coming online. These units were launched and sold preconstruction over the past half-dozen years. Now they're being delivered, and their volume is one reason Panama's capital city's market continues to be soft.

- **The Path of Progress.** Easier and better access opens up locations to broader markets. Therefore, one way to choose a market for investment is to identify a place where some important infrastructure improvement is planned. A new airport, train station, highway, hospital, and so on, can mean a new universe of potential buyers. A newly paved road, for example, that cuts travel time in half, can make a location more accessible and therefore more valuable. All these things can translate into an exit strategy for an investor looking to develop or to flip.

- **Opportunity for Diversification.** Diversification pertains to market, type of investment, type of property, and currency. A rental apartment in Medellín gives you an asset in Colombia that could generate cash flow in Colombian pesos. An agricultural investment in Brazil means another asset type, another economy, another currency, and so on. The important thing to understand on the topic of diversification is that owning different kinds of properties in various cities and states across the United States isn't diversification. It's being invested in the United States.

    However, moving all your real estate investment capital out of the United States and placing it in any other single market—Panama, for example, or Colombia or Brazil—does not qualify as diversification either. Many investors I speak with recognize that holding property investments in two or three different U.S. cities means they are still fully exposed and vulnerable to U.S. market and U.S. dollar risks. Many, though, don't see that selling off all U.S. assets and reinvesting the capital in property in a single other country, even if, again, in different kinds of properties in different cities or locations throughout that single other country, is a similarly vulnerable position.

The point of diversification is to make sure you are not at the mercy of any single market, economy, political landscape, government, or currency. A global property diversification strategy may or may not include investments in the United States, but it must include investments in at least two (and preferably at least three) countries, ideally each with its own currency.

Note that not all foreign property markets bring currency diversification, because some countries use the U.S. dollar (Panama and Ecuador); some have their currencies pegged to the U.S. dollar (Belize); and, in some countries, although they have their own currency, real estate is traded in U.S. dollars (Nicaragua), meaning that your currency hedge isn't as clean as it could be.

One more thing about investing in real estate overseas for currency diversification: Don't try to time it. You can't, not in the long-term and not in the short-term either, which is why I recommend, when shopping for a property purchase overseas, that you pay less attention to currency movements and more attention to property values. It's impossible to know which way any currency is going to move day to day. In the meantime, while you're trying to time the currency, the property market is moving, too.

If you know that you're interested in a particular market and the local currency takes a sudden hit, you could take that opportunity to move money in anticipation of making a buy. However, while waiting for the currency to do what you want it to, you run the risk of missing out on a good investment just because the time isn't "right" from a currency point of view. You can't time when you'll find the piece of property that you're searching for unless you don't allow yourself to begin looking until the currency moves to where you want it. That's a backward approach. Locking in a good deal on a property is much better than worrying too much about a few percentage points on a currency move that may or may not happen according to your timeline.

- **Costs of Acquisition and Disposal.** Remember that these, which I refer to as the round-trip costs of making an investment, go beyond agent commissions and vary dramatically from country to country. This is an important thing to research and understand in full no matter why you're making a purchase. However, investor-buyers who underestimate or underplan for the costs of acquisition and of eventually reselling can undermine their investment before making it. Depending on the market, the costs of purchasing a piece of real estate in another country can include—in addition to agent commissions—the following: legal fees, notary fees, registration fees, title insurance, and transfer taxes (sometimes called stamp duty). In Ireland, for example, stamp duty was as much as 9 percent of the purchase price when we bought, payable in cash upon closing and not a cost you wanted to overlook in your budgeting. (Today it's 1 percent if the purchase price is less than 1 million euro.)

Again, though, remember, we're talking not only about the costs of acquisition, but the round-trip costs of a purchase. Exiting comes at a cost, too. When selling, you may have another agent commission to pay, and you'll likely have additional attorney fees. These are usually minimal, even negligible. The more significant cost associated with exiting a foreign property investment can be the tax hit. I discuss strategies for how to figure and how to minimize this in Part IV.

The total round-trip costs of investing in a piece of real estate overseas can range from a few percentage points to more than 25 percent at the extreme and that can be before taking into account capital gains taxes.

• **Carrying Costs.** These costs include maintenance (a house on the beach requires a lot of it); a caretaker (if necessary); property taxes (not every country charges them, and, in some countries, they're negligible); income taxes (if you're earning rental income); capital gains taxes (when you eventually resell; again, not every country charges them); other local taxes; property management expense (you'll need a property manager if you intend to rent); rental management expense (separate from property management and necessary unless you're going to manage your rental investment yourself, something I don't advise); and homeowner's association/building/condo fees.

3

Buy Overseas to Save Your Retirement

About 600,000 American retirees have their Social Security payments direct-deposited into foreign banks or receive their monthly checks at foreign addresses, and the U.S. State Department reports about 6.3 million Americans living abroad. Those 6.3 million Americans abroad are the ones voluntarily reporting their status to U.S. embassies, and many thousands of retirees living overseas continue to have their Social Security payments deposited to U.S. bank accounts (because it's easier). In other words, there's no way to know for sure how many American retirees are retired beyond U.S. borders, but I can tell you one thing about this with certainty: The number is growing fast.

The current plight of the American retiree is well known. The baby boomer retirees, having worked hard, funded a retirement account, invested in a home, raised a family, and dreamed of the day it would all pay off, are right now facing the reality that things aren't working out as they'd long hoped. Maybe their retirement account is worth half (or less) what they expected it'd be worth at this point. Maybe their home is worth half what they were counting on, too, or, worse, maybe they owe more on the home mortgage than the property could reasonably be expected to sell for. Maybe, bottom line, their retirement resources aren't adequate to fund the retirement they were looking forward to.

If you're at or approaching this stage of life yourself, you understand the concerns all too well, and you're likely worried, maybe even panicked, over your future. How can you avoid giving up on your long-held dream retirement lifestyle? Thinking more practically, how can you make sure you don't outlive your retirement nest egg?

Two words: Retire overseas.

It's possible to retire comfortably in a number of beautiful, friendly, safe, pleasant destinations on a budget of $1,200 per month or less. Coincidentally, that's just about the amount of the average monthly Social Security check, meaning that it isn't exaggerating the point to say that it's possible for the average American to retire overseas on his or her Social Security alone. It's also possible to retire in the United States on Social Security alone. It must be, because many Americans are doing it. The question is, what standard of living can retirees afford on Social Security alone stateside, especially if their Social Security check amounts to but $1,200 or less each month? Generally speaking, the answer is not a great one.

This leads to the other primary reason to consider relocating abroad in retirement—to improve your quality of life. Dollar for dollar, the lifestyle your retirement budget could buy you in dozens of places around the world will be richer, fuller, and more interesting than the lifestyle that budget could buy you in the United States. Retiring overseas, this phase of life shifts from being a cause for concern to the adventure of your lifetime. I make this claim based on almost three decades of experience watching and helping Americans (thousands of them) retire to other countries.

Retiring to another country means moving completely outside your comfort zone. It requires an open mind, a ready sense of humor, and a willingness to accept, at this later stage of life, that you don't know everything, that you've still got much to learn. Retiring overseas means starting over. That's terrifying, maybe, but ultimately and more important, it's also an opportunity for personal renaissance. Sure, your costs of housing and of health care will be reduced and you'll maybe be able to dine out as often as you like, but more interesting big picture, retiring overseas also means you're making new friends, forming a new circle of support, seeing new places, experiencing new things, and maybe learning a new language. At an age when others are considering returning to the workforce as Wal-Mart greeters in desperate attempts to pay their winter heating bills, you could be taking off for exotic, sun-drenched shores where heating is altogether unnecessary any time of year.

A migration is taking place. It began, quietly, on the fringes, perhaps two and a half decades ago, but now it's building momentum and making its way on to mainstream America's radar. The Associated Press, the AARP, the *New*

York Times, and *USA Today* have all reported on it. I call it the Retirement Revolution. If you're an investor, you can position yourself ahead of this migration to profit in the markets these wandering retirees are making. If you're a retiree, you'd do well to think about joining the march.

The case for considering launching your retirement overseas is strong. That's not my point here. My point here is that once you've decided to launch your retirement overseas, you're going to need a place to live wherever "overseas" turns out to be for you. In this context, you're not buying for investment. You're buying for retirement. As a retiree-buyer, your purchase decision should be led not by path of progress assessments, cash flow projections, capital return expectations, or currency movements, not by anything cognitive or quantifiable, but by your heart and your gut.

When retirees decide to take their retirement global, one of the first big questions they face is, where? Not only where in the world (as in what country might be best for you), but also where to reside: A house? An apartment? A gated community? In fact, though, the question at first shouldn't be where to buy a retirement residence overseas. The question at first for the retiree-buyer should be: Should you *buy* a retirement residence overseas at all?

Owning versus Renting

If your overseas real estate agenda is purely to do with finding a place to live in retirement in a foreign country, maybe it's not a real estate purchase you want but a rental.

For each of my three international moves—from Baltimore, Maryland, to Waterford, Ireland; from Waterford to Paris; and then, most recently, in 2008, from Paris to Panama City, Panama—we've rented first and been glad we did. In each case, we discovered that the place where we settled initially wasn't the place where we really wanted to be. In Waterford, we realized we didn't want to be in the city but outside it so that we could savor Irish country living. In Paris, it was a matter of a dozen blocks or so, but that distance made the difference between being at the heart of the chaos come tourist season each year and being hidden away and removed from it while still having the best of central Paris on our doorstep. In Panama City, we've relocated three times before finally finding the neighborhood where we feel the most comfortable.

Panama City is a good example because, for such a small city, the diversity of lifestyle options is great, and neighborhoods just a mile or two away from each other make for dramatically different living experiences. Buying before giving yourself a chance to understand this can mean the difference between loving your new life overseas and regretting it. Thinking more practically, depending on the country where you're retiring, the costs of buying and reselling property can be significant, meaning that buying wrong can be expensive.

On the other hand, I can imagine circumstances when you might choose to ignore my "rent first" caveat and buy from the start of your retire overseas adventure. If you're retiring to a place where property values are appreciating, waiting a year before buying means you could be passing up healthy gains. Remember, the market dynamics that attracted you are attracting others, and early buyers enjoy the highest rates of appreciation.

Rent-Free Retirement

Buying real estate overseas is fundamentally about diversification. This is true whether you buy for investment or for retirement and it argues in favor of buying for retirement rather than renting. Buying your new retirement residence overseas means moving money out of the United States and putting it into another market and, potentially, another currency. Moving all your money out of the States and into a new retirement residence overseas doesn't alone bring you the diversification you should be seeking right now. However, using some of your capital to purchase a retirement residence in the place where you want to live and putting another portion of your capital to work in another market (that perhaps uses a different currency) gets you not only diversification but also what amounts to a rent-free retirement.

Another advantage of buying your retirement residence overseas rather than renting it is that it helps you take the plunge. It allows you to move your life forward, unequivocally, embracing the new adventure. Many who rent before they buy do so to be able to maintain a property back home, just in case. Although this can be sensible, it's also an anchor, a drag. It can divide your attention and keep you looking backward instead of ahead to your new life. Keeping one foot on the pier and the other on the departing boat can land you in the drink. You may remain only partially committed, which will be a handicap.

The bottom line for the retiree-buyer is to follow your instincts, not only with regard to what to buy overseas but also when answering the question of whether you should buy at all. You know yourself, your motivations and preferences, and how well you've researched your chosen destination. You know your level of commitment, your level of readiness, and your tolerance for risk.

How to Buy for Retirement

If you're buying real estate for personal use in retirement, you want to think about things like:

- How much space will you need? Do you want an apartment or a house? One bedroom or two? (You probably won't need more than two.) Two levels or only one? A guest room or even a guesthouse? Will you have guests often, for example? Will you want them to be able to stay with you, or would you prefer if they came and went from a hotel nearby?
- Do you want a front yard, a back garden, or a swimming pool? All of these things require care and maintenance.
- Do you want to be in the heart of downtown or out in the country?
- Do you want a turnkey, a renovation project, or something in between?
- Do you like the idea of living in a gated community, or would you prefer a more integrated setting, such as a neighborhood where you could become part of the local community? This is a key consideration. Going local means you have to learn the local language (if you don't speak it already). Or perhaps you'd prefer to be off on your own with undeveloped acres between you and your nearest neighbor. In this type of rural setting you will need to build your own in-case-of-emergency infrastructure.
- Consider traffic patterns and transportation. Where you base yourself determines whether you'll need to invest in a car, which is an important budget consideration.
- Consider the convenience factor. How far is it to shopping, restaurants, nightlife, parking, and the nearest medical facility?
- Do you want a furnished home? You may have no choice but to buy unfurnished (unless you buy, say, from other expats who are interested in selling their place including all contents). Buying unfurnished means

you'll need to purchase furniture locally or ship your household goods from home.

- What's your budget? This is the most practical guideline of all, of course. Be clear on your finances before you start shopping, and, if your budget is strict, don't be tempted to consider properties outside your price point. You'll only be disappointing yourself unnecessarily.
- Finally, ask yourself what kind of view you'd like from your bedroom window each morning. This can be an effective way to focus on something important that might otherwise be overlooked until it's too late.

Are You Ready to Go Local? (If Yes, You Could Retire Well on as Little as $700 per Month)

It's possible to retire overseas and live well on a budget of as little as $700 per month. That's an extreme, though, and it's not to say that you could retire anywhere overseas on $700 per month. The choices that meet this criterion have something else in common—they can all also be described as "local" options. By this I mean these are places where you'd be living like the locals, among the locals, shopping where the locals shop, eating where the locals eat, and speaking whatever language the locals speak. Top options for where to retire well today on a strictly limited budget include Ecuador, Nicaragua, Thailand, and Vietnam. Thailand and Vietnam are not places I'd recommend for real estate investment. In Vietnam, in fact, it's not possible for foreigners to purchase land or a residence.

The two best places right now, therefore, to consider combining the budget retiree-buyer agenda with the investor-buyer agenda are Ecuador and Nicaragua. Specifically, I'd recommend looking at Cuenca (colonial city) or Cotacachi (mountain town) in Ecuador and Granada (oldest colonial city in the Americas) in Nicaragua. In Cuenca, you could buy a retirement residence in the center of town for as little as $850 per square meter. That's absolutely, universally cheap. It means that a 150-square-meter house or apartment (that's about 1,500 square feet), at one of the city's most central addresses, in move-in condition, can be had for as little as $125,000. In Cotacachi, you could own for less, as little as $600 per square meter. Life in Cotacachi wouldn't be for everyone. This is rural, remote Ecuador, and

Ecuador is a Third World country where you won't forget you're in a Third World country. Still, you could own your own retirement residence here, with beautiful mountainscapes all around, for well under $100,000, and you could live in it comfortably on a budget of even $500 or $600 a month. You aren't going to match the quality of life you could enjoy in this part of Ecuador on such a minimal budget anywhere else in the world.

Nicaragua in general is slightly more expensive than Ecuador, but the costs both of living and of real estate in Granada in particular are on par with those in Cuenca. One big difference between these two retirement options is that, in Granada, you're retired at sea level (although on the shores of a lake, not the ocean), while in Cuenca, you're in the mountains. Your choice could come down to the kind of climate you're looking for.

I'll offer two more budget-retiree choices that also present good investor-buyer opportunities. These options don't fit into the "retire on less than $700 per month" category, but they are my top recommendations for where to retire on a modest budget if Third World living isn't for you. Not everyone is cut out for life in the tropics or the developing world. If your retirement dream is more about the good life in the Old World, I'd suggest you look at rural France (not Provence, but west of there) or rural Italy (not Florence, but south and east of that well-known and, yes, too-expensive-for-the-retiree-on-a-budget locale). Specifically, in France's Béarn region and in Italy's Abruzzo, you could enjoy the best of country life on the continent on a budget that qualifies as small (as little as $1,200 per month), and at the same time you would be combining an idyllic, Old World retirement lifestyle with an investment in a euro-denominated real asset that would provide diversification, the potential for appreciation, and a nice inheritance for your heirs. In both these regions you could buy a home of your own for as little as 1,000 euro per square meter. Considered in the context of what you're buying and where, that is a very good price.

Meters and Measures

I'll stop here to explain my per-square-meter references. In nearly all the world outside the United States, this is how real estate is measured. One square meter equals 10.76 square feet. For purposes of rough calculations in your head, you can multiply or divide, as the case may be, by 10.

I recommend that as you consider venturing off into the world of overseas property, you make this adjustment. Get your head around meters instead of feet and train yourself to process every piece of real estate you consider in that context. It's the best way to compare properties and prices. As there are no multiple listing services outside North America, you're going to have to make your own comparisons. The only way to do this is to use standard units of measure.

On the subject of measurements, also note that in much of the world land is measured not in acres but hectares. A hectare is equal to 2.47 acres. In Nicaragua, Costa Rica, and sometimes in Argentina, land is measured in *manzanas*. In Nicaragua, a *manzana* is equal to 1.74 acres; in Costa Rica, it's 1.727 acres; and in Argentina, a *manzana* is a hectare. In Thailand, land is measured in *rais;* 1 *rai* is 0.395 of an acre. You can make these kinds of conversions easily at www.onlineconversion.com/area.htm.

Three Places to Live the American Retirement Dream Overseas

I've offered recommendations for where to combine the retiree-buyer's agenda with that of the investor-buyer if your retirement budget is very small or if you're interested in "going local" and embracing a local lifestyle. However, local living overseas isn't for everyone. Perhaps you like the idea of stretching your retirement dollars as far as possible, reducing your cost of living and of health care, while at the same time enriching and enhancing your quality of life, but you're not up for learning a new language or putting up with the day-to-day challenges and frustrations of life in the developing world. Don't despair. In a handful of places overseas that have emerged in recent years as top expat havens, it's possible to enjoy many of the advantages of being retired overseas without having to cross over to a local lifestyle. These are places where the American Dream has been exported and where the day-to-day living probably resembles what you left behind back home.

Three top choices for exporting the American Dream with you when you retire overseas are Boquete, Panama; San Pedro, Ambergris Caye, Belize; and Puerto Vallarta, Mexico. In each of these places, communities of foreign, mostly American, retirees have developed and are expanding. Living in Boquete (in the highlands of Panama, meaning cool and even chilly temperatures year-round and beautiful mountain and river views), in San Pedro (a former fishing village that has grown into a small beach town with cafés, art galleries, wine shops, and expat clubs), or in Puerto Vallarta (the most affordable place in the world to live what I'd describe as a luxury coastal lifestyle, complete with marinas, yacht clubs, golf courses, and fine dining), you could be retired overseas (enjoying affordable and top-quality health care, an affordable cost of living, and the adventure of starting over somewhere new), but you wouldn't have to learn to speak Spanish if you didn't want to (Ambergris Caye is part of Belize, and the folks in Belize all speak English anyway). You could buy your groceries in shops that likely resemble places where you shopped back home. You could eat out several times every week, choosing from Italian, French, or Asian cuisine, even sushi. You could start your day with gourmet coffee served by a smiling, friendly clerk accustomed to serving English-speaking customers. You could play bridge on Thursday nights and go golfing (in Boquete or Puerto Vallarta) or fishing (in San Pedro or Puerto Vallarta) every Sunday morning, all in the company of English speakers.

Each of these three places is also a reasonable or better choice for investing in real estate overseas, meaning that these are again good options for combining the retiree-buyer's agenda with that of the investor-buyer. Further, Boquete, San Pedro, and Puerto Vallarta are all also great places to go on holiday, meaning that they qualify as ultimate-buyer destinations, presenting the opportunity to achieve all three overseas real estate agendas with a single purchase.

4 Buy Overseas to Make Travel and Adventure Part of Your Life Right Now

But haven't we done this already? Haven't we already bought an old stone house surrounded by mud? Isn't that what we just did in Ireland? Why do you guys want to do this again?"

In 2004, my husband, Lief, our two children, and I spent a week touring around Istria, Croatia, with a focused agenda. We were in the market for one of the old white stone houses you find across this peninsula. To that end, Kaitlin, 15; Jackson, 5; Lief; and I, in one car, followed our property agent, in her car, from one stone farmhouse to another, up and down the narrow winding roads of these mountainsides, through the medieval villages, and past the ever-present fields of olive trees, grape vines, and sunflowers.

We had recently made our move, from Ireland to France, and one rainy morning of that Istrian family adventure, standing in one more muddy Istrian farmyard, Kaitlin made the observation I share at the opening of this chapter. Probably she wasn't the only one wondering what in the world we were doing. Having just relocated to Paris, where we were still in the process of renovating the apartment that would be our home in that city, busy with other business and investment projects, why had we gotten it into our heads that we wanted to buy a 200-year-old house on the side of a mountain in the middle of the Istrian Peninsula?

Because we liked it there. We wanted to stake our small claim to this beautiful and historic region that, during previous visits, in previous years, had captured our hearts and imaginations. We believed in the future of Croatia, a country with an extraordinarily complicated past and an extremely open-minded, forward-looking population. We recognized at the time that Croatia was at another turning point in its long history, and we wanted to be part of it.

Plus, the Istrian Peninsula, we'd observed for some time, serves up some of the most delightful scenery on the planet. The land seems to rise up to embrace you. Everywhere you look, something nice is growing—olives, grapes, figs, tomatoes, pumpkins, blackberries, wildflowers . . . Even the buildings seem to be of the earth, built of its white stone and red clay. In some parts of the world, Nature outdoes herself. In others, that which man has built is impressive. In Istria, Nature and mankind have worked together over centuries, starting with the Romans, to create a land of delights you have to see to appreciate.

So, that rainy morning in that muddy farmyard with Kaitlin (and I'm sure others, too) questioning our sense, Lief and I decided that we'd found the old white stone house that fit our bill, made an offer to the Istrian owner, and agreed to the terms with a handshake. The seller sealed the deal by making a gift to us of lavender oil that his wife had bottled.

Before you're ready to retire, you're likely to notice places around the world where you'd like to be able to spend time. Not just once every several years or so in a hotel, but more regularly, as often as possible, in the company of your family and friends, and in a place of your own. That's the realization we made years ago in Istria, Croatia.

When you identify a destination that meets this description, I recommend that you take stock of it in a bigger-picture way, considering first whether that destination is also a place where you think you might like to spend time in retirement, and second, if the real estate market there presents potential for capital appreciation or cash flow. If the answer to either of those questions is yes (and certainly if the answer to both of those questions is yes), then you've found your ideal second home overseas.

In our case, with Istria, the answer to both those taking-stock questions was enthusiastically positive, and so we proceeded with the purchase. While the house we bought in Waterford and the apartment we bought in Paris were purchased because we needed places to live with our family at the time, the property in Istria was bought because we'd decided that this region was a part of the world where we wanted an excuse to return as often as we could manage. In addition, Lief and I agreed that this was also a place we could see ourselves coming back to longer term, a place that could become part of our eventual retirement plan.

When it comes time to flip the switch to retirement, Lief and I hope to have organized our lives so that we're able to move around during that phase of life among a handful of destinations where we most enjoy spending time, with established infrastructure in each so that we can come and go as residents, not tourists, with friends and connections, social circles and, important to us, homes of our own. When making your own plan for retirement overseas, the starting-point key to the success of the adventure is to be honest with yourself as to what kind of lifestyle you're after. When Lief and I ask ourselves what kind of lifestyle we want in retirement, the answer is varied. City and coastal, Caribbean and highland, spring and summer, fall and winter, developed and emerging, sophisticated and raw, refined and gritty, we appreciate it all. So we've conceived a retirement plan, that we've been working for the past 15 years to engineer, that will allow us to enjoy it all, perpetually, in turns. We've held on to the apartment in Paris that we called home when we lived in that city with our children. This will be our retirement base. From Paris, we'll enjoy regular extended trips to Istria, to stay in the farmhouse there; to Medellín, Colombia, to enjoy life in that sophisticated mountain city; and to the Pacific coast of Panama, where we're building a beach house. This is an ambitious plan (some might say ridiculously so), but we've had time to develop it.

Whatever your plan, I encourage you to start developing it as soon as possible. An easy first step can be the purchase of a piece of property in a locale where you want to be able to spend time now and that you think eventually could become part of your retirement plan. Meantime, whenever you're not using the property yourself, it could be generating cash flow from rental, and, over time, it could be increasing in value, too. Your future retirement residence could be a nicely appreciating asset on your balance sheet.

As we've been discussing, that's the ideal situation—when the holiday home-cum-retirement plan you buy also qualifies as an investment. This was what tipped the scales for us with the farmhouse purchase in Istria. The old farmhouse we bought came with a bit of land. On that land, we daydreamed of cultivating olives, figs, even grapes. Maybe we could try making our own wine! We could go for long hikes in the hills, exploring the nearby medieval villages by day, and then read by firelight come evening. We'd return to these ideas again and again and, finally, rationalized them with the agreement that this was a market we believed in. Croatians, we noted, were tired of struggling and fighting. They wanted peace and prosperity and were working hard to rebuild their country. Croatia's investment in infrastructure was and continues to be substantial, including an extensive modern highway system that allows you to travel through and across this mountainous country efficiently and comfortably thanks to a network of tunnels and bridges that is an engineering marvel. Lief and I like countries at turning points, because they're lands of opportunity. That's how we perceived Croatia when we made our purchase there, meaning we believed an investment in real estate in that country at that time positioned us for long-term capital appreciation. The growing tourist markets in Croatia, and especially in the region of Istria where we bought (thanks to annual film and truffles festivals), meant as well an opportunity for the property to generate cash flow when we weren't using it ourselves. In addition, we were buying in a country where real estate trades in euro, furthering our diversification agenda.

Sizing Up a Holiday Home/Vacation Rental Buy

What's specifically important when sizing up a potential second home overseas? You're buying primarily for personal use, so the driving consideration should be the pleasure potential for you and your family. Buy what and where you want. Balance that objective, though, against what matters most for rentals in your chosen market, because one important objective for any holiday home is that you're able to rent it out when you're not using it, generating enough cash flow to cover associated carrying costs and, ideally, leaving something left over each year (positive cash flow) to boot.

Property type and size are universally important rental factors. In most markets, a one- or two-bedroom property is more rentable than a three- or four-bedroom place. The incrementally higher rental rates you should be able to charge for a three-bedroom usually don't compensate for the higher cost of purchasing the larger apartment. Although a super-high-end property might suit your personal preferences, a higher-end (read: more expensive) property probably means a lower rental return. To keep your occupancy up, you'll likely have to compete on price with the general (not high-end) market.

Here are questions to answer when considering any potential second home/vacation rental overseas purchase:

- Where in your target location do people most want to stay? In Paris, for example, perhaps the world's most recession-proof rentals market, the traditionally best *arrondissements* for rental are the fifth and sixth. These are also among the most costly *arrondissements*. More affordable and also good for rental are the fourth and the ninth *arrondissements,* meaning an investment in these areas could generate better cash flow.

Take a similar approach when shopping for a rental in any city. Rather than focusing on the heart of the most rentable district, look around the fringes of the main tourist area and work your numbers to determine whether the lower acquisition costs could result in a better cash flow, even with slightly lower expectations for rental price and occupancy.

When shopping for a rental in a beach location, the closer to the beach the better (obviously). However, again, prices will be higher right at the beach so something slightly removed with an ocean view might be a better buy.

- What sizes of rentals are in demand in your target market? Again, generally speaking, one- and two-bedroom apartments are the rental sweet spot. However, a market can be overrun with rentals of this size, creating opportunities for either smaller (studios, for example) or bigger (three-bedroom) places.

    In Medellín, investors are buying two- and three-bedroom apartments, even if that's more apartment than they need, because the prices are so low it's hard not to be tempted to buy bigger and, right now, rental returns for these apartments are high. That said, a one-bedroom apartment in this city could generate the same or better cash flow. Again, it's a matter of balancing investment agenda with personal circumstances and preferences.

- Is there a high season and what's the opportunity for occupancy beyond that time? Also, when considering the rental season, remember your plan (if you have one) for personal use. Would you want to be occupying the place yourself during the season when much of your rental return otherwise might be earned?

    Punta del Este, Uruguay, is a good case study in this context. The high season in this coastal resort town is mid-December through February. Over this 10-week window, you can charge outrageous rental rates. In fact, it's not uncommon to earn as much as 80 or 90 percent of the annual rental income during this peak-season period alone. The rest of the year, the going rental rates are a fraction of the short-term rents you can ask in January and February. That's okay, as you can earn enough during this period to make the investment worthwhile overall. Unless, of course, that's the time of year you'd want to use the place yourself. In that case, your intended rental investment could default into a holiday home for the family, period.

How to Target Where to Buy

Five Strategies for Choosing a Property Market Overseas

I was in Montenegro researching the property market in that country in 2005. One real estate agent who toured me around told a story of a buyer she had worked with the previous week. The client was a young Irish girl, a hairdresser from Dublin who had decided she should get in on the worldwide real estate boom. She couldn't afford anything back home, as Ireland was already well overpriced (especially, I guess, for a young girl earning a hairdresser's salary), so she'd targeted Montenegro, a recognized up-and-coming market at the time. The real estate agent showed the girl several properties. When she walked through the door of one apartment, the Irish girl exclaimed, "It's perfect. I'll take it. How much is it?"

That's how nutty the global property scene was back then. Everyone was afraid of missing out. The thinking was, buy now and understand what you're doing later, a naïve and dangerous strategy predicated on two notions—first, that real estate prices could never do anything but continue up, and second, that a buyer would never have trouble finding another buyer when the time came to sell.

It's a very different world today, and a reverse risk is emerging. In the current climate of bargains and distress sales, the investor-buyer must avoid thinking, "With prices this low, how can I go wrong?" If you're looking for a place to live or retire, that's one thing, but if you're buying with expectation of return, cheap doesn't necessarily mean a good buy and it certainly doesn't automatically translate to a profitable investment, especially if the market is driven more by foreign than local buyers. Foreign, especially foreign American, buyers can be thin on the ground in much of the world these days.

You don't make money when you sell real estate but when you buy it. Buy wrong, and the likelihood of a successful experience is greatly diminished. A big part of buying right is to understand your eventual exit strategy. Will you sell? When? Rent? To whom?

When deciding where to buy, you also want to understand the market forces at work. Why are prices so deflated? Is there some reason to believe they will appreciate in some identifiable period? Who is buying? Who might be buying in the future? Why? The most appealing property investments are those that are undervalued on a global scale (that is, they are cheap relative to comparable real estate other places), but that reside in markets with strong underlying fundamentals and positive economic upsides, meaning you can have some reasonable expectation of finding a buyer when you eventually decide you want one.

The most interesting overseas real estate opportunities today are to be found in countries in crisis. Let's start there.

5 Buy Crisis Opportunity

For a while in the 1990s and through the middle of the first decade of this century, property investors the world over believed that values only went up. In 2008, we all were reminded that all markets move in cycles, both up and down, sometimes spectacularly down. If you can identify a country in a down cycle, understand why property values there have fallen, and conceive an exit strategy that makes sense in the context of what's gone wrong, how long the down market might continue, and your own agendas, both investment and lifestyle, then you can be in a position to make what likely will prove both the smartest and the most successful real estate buys of both your investor career and your lifetime.

Crisis Buy 1: Argentina—The World's Most Experienced Crisis Market

The world's best example of a crisis market is Argentina. More than any other country, Argentina goes through wild cycles, slingshotting property values up and down. To understand how the going got so weird in this country, you have to think back to populist politician Juan Perón. Perón took over Argentina in 1946 and pretty much destroyed the country's productive sector. As you might guess, with such wanton destruction to his credit, Perón remains the most popular political figure in Argentina today.

Perón introduced the concept of a national wage increase. He'd go on radio and announce that as of the following month workers were to be paid

20 percent more (or whatever). Typically prices would then go up more than 20 percent, giving rise to the Argentine expression that wages go up by the stairway, prices by the elevator. When workers finally collected their higher wages, they discovered they had less purchasing power, not more. So Perón would then come up with a new plan—another 20 percent wage increase, but this time with price controls. Businesses had to pay their workers a lot more but maintain the same selling prices.

Perón's policy promptly led to shortages in everything from bread to gasoline, from tools to clothes. To deal with the shortages, Perón came up with a third idea: the Law of Supply. The Law of Supply, still on the books today, says that if you're in the pizza business, say, you have to continue to make pizzas no matter what. Specifically, if the cost to make a pizza comes to 100 pesos and the maximum price permitted by the Peronists is 60 pesos, you must continue to make pizzas anyway and suffer the loss of 40 pesos per pizza. The Law of Supply provides that, in the event the government catches you *not* making pizzas, it can confiscate your assets.

Perón invented other laws, too. He came up with an official list of names, for example. You had to name your baby one of the names on the list. So Dennis became Dionissimo on your birth certificate, even though your parents call you Dennis and you may be unable to speak Spanish.

Perón also required speaking Spanish, and no other language, on international phone calls. The country had only a few overseas lines in those days, and operators could easily monitor calls. A friend tells the story of calling his boss in Uruguay one day. He and his boss struggled with Spanish, but the law was the law. They fumbled and faked their way through, speaking Spanish as best they could, which was not good at all. Finally the operator interrupted. "Gentlemen, you must speak Spanish."

"But we are speaking Spanish!"

Perón came up with the original *vedas*, or prohibitions, on eating meat or bread or whatever. Say the price of meat was going up too fast. Perón would then make it illegal to sell or serve meat on a given day, say Tuesdays. He figured by lowering the demand for meat by one-seventh, prices would fall. Supply and demand, remember? *Vedas* never worked, for reasons you can guess, but that didn't prevent successive governments from trying them.

At one time, the price of meat went up so much that the government of the day banned meat on Thursdays. After a few months of experience with the *veda*, someone asked the Minister of Economy if it had helped to reduce the price of meat. "We can't tell," said the minister, "but we're continuing the *veda* anyway."

Argentina's military threw Perón out in 1955. Perón wound up in Madrid, plotting his return. Among other activities, he allegedly armed a guerrilla group, the Montoneros. Perón figured Argentina might become such a mess that he'd be invited back. It worked. In 1974 Perón made a triumphant return to Buenos Aires and had himself elected president. He intended to deal with the rival gangs that continued to ravage the country, but before he got around to it, he died. His second wife, Isabelita (Evita was his first wife), succeeded him as president until March 1976, when the military again took over.

Friend Paul Terhorst and his wife, Vicki, moved from San Francisco to Buenos Aires five years later, in 1981. As Paul explains, "The military junta that had thrown out Isabelita was still in power. Their program of 'disappearing' thousands of terrorists, friends of terrorists, people with names of terrorists in their phone books, and people with names of nonterrorists in their phone books who the government guessed were terrorists was winding down. On the economic front Argentina was going through a period of *plata dulce*, or easy money. Easy money meant an overvalued peso and expensive real estate."

Paul and Vicki's arrival date in Argentina in 1981 serves as a good time to talk about this country's boom/bust real estate cycle. As Paul explains, "When Vicki and I arrived on the scene, I was still working. Like most young-comers, I figured I should buy an apartment upon arrival. That's what you do when you're young, right? Buy real estate in a good location and live there forever."

"My savvy, sophisticated Argentine boss flat refused to let me buy into such a hot market," Paul continues. "He'd lived the Perón boom, the Perón bust, the military bust, the military boom. 'The market here is way too dicey,' he told me. 'I bought an apartment many years ago for $100,000,' he explained. 'My place has been worth as much as $350,000, as little as $50,000. Right now we're at the high end of the scale, no way should you buy.'

"I figured he knew what he was talking about, so, instead of buying, Vicki and I rented an apartment. Argentina proceeded to fall apart. In our first year there we lived through four *coups d'etat*, multiple devaluations, and an economic collapse, all accompanied by a sharp fall in real estate prices. We were glad we hadn't bought."

Government policies in Argentina since 2005 have driven up inflation, without relief in the exchange rate. Friends had a small house outside Buenos Aires. When they bought, the annual costs to maintain the house (security, gardening, maintenance, and taxes) amounted to about $2,000 a year. By 2011, those costs had been inflated to $20,000 a year. Ouch. "I saw those costs going much higher soon," my friend told me. He sold the house in January 2012, just in time.

Later in 2012 Argentina's president Cristina Fernandez prohibited most legal sales of dollars. Since Argentines need dollars to buy real estate, real estate transactions plummeted. A black market for dollars quickly surfaced, but the government comes down hard on dealers. Getting dollars into Argentina today, and especially getting them out of Argentina, is expensive.

Cristina admires Juan Perón. She says she never makes a decision without first asking herself what Perón would do. She's moved beyond *vedas* and national wage increases, though, and beyond an official list of names. In Cristina's Argentina you can speak on the phone in your preferred language. Call it progress of sorts.

Cristina, though, seems intent on curtailing economic freedom, which she deeply distrusts. She punishes overseas travel, prohibits most imports, and confiscates so much of the soybean crop that producers lose money. She relies on price controls, currency bans, and dividend approvals to keep the economy under her thumb. She nationalized Aerolíneas Argentinas. She's even taken over Argentine football.

If she dislikes the results of her policies, she covers them up. She falsifies inflation numbers, for example. The *CIA Factbook*, perhaps the world's most careful, politically correct source for this type of information, uses private estimates of inflation in this country rather than the trumped-up government figures. In addition, because of high crime rates, Cristina has avoided publishing crime reports for four years.

I predict that Cristina will be able to maintain control—to kick the can down the road—for quite some time. She's good at managing fiscal cash flow; she knows that other governments collapsed because leaders ran out of money. She'll make sure that her net cash flow stays reliable. High soybean and corn prices, mainly due to drought in the United States, continue to fill government coffers. Cristina has imposed new travel taxes, and I predict she'll eventually raise the departure tax and require that Argentines get approval from the tax authorities before being allowed to fly overseas.

One key indicator of Cristina's future will be the Law of Supply. Cristina threatens to enforce the Law of Supply from time to time but thus far really has not. If she goes ahead with the Law of Supply and actively shuts down producers big and small for refusing to operate at a loss, she'll be desperate. The end will be near.

As of this writing, real estate prices in this country remain a mystery. Buenos Aires apartments now sell in dollars, yet Cristina has prohibited buying those dollars or using those dollars to buy apartments. She's insisting that buyers and sellers operate in pesos, which few players want to do. So for the time being we're seeing few transactions and would-be buyers can only guess about trends in prices.

I predict the economic and real estate environment in Argentina will continue to deteriorate, probably for some time, before things collapse. Have patience. Wait for a full-blown crash before going in.

Crisis Buy 2: Ireland—Bust to Boom to Bust in a Single Generation

Denis, a young Irish friend, relocated recently from Dublin to Panama City to join my Live and Invest Overseas editorial team. When I asked him about the move, he explained, flat: "I'm here because my own country is a mess."

Denis went on: "I remember being 16 in high school history class. Our teacher was trying to explain to us that our country was facing potential economic troubles, that bad things lay ahead for us. He predicted a return to tough times for Ireland. We all rolled our eyes and made jokes. We didn't believe Ireland could suffer economically, not anymore, not again. All we had ever known was economic growth. Stories about no work, no money—all that was ancient history. Boy, were we in for a rude awakening not too many years later."

Denis, a lad of but 21 years, was born into the Celtic Tiger age. For him and his fellows, Ireland was a land of plenty. All their early lives, everywhere, they knew plenty of money, plenty of work, plenty of construction, plenty of credit, plenty of optimism, even plenty of arrogance. Somehow, over the past 25 years, the Irish became convinced that Ireland was an economic power-house with unlimited stores of potential. This period of Irish history, it's worth pointing out, is unique in all Irish history. Never before had any Irish generation known such prosperity.

When we moved to Ireland in the mid-1990s, real estate prices across the country had already been appreciating by as much as 15 to 25 percent a year for a few years running. What was driving the growth, we'd ask people. "Ah, it's the Celtic Tiger," they'd tell us. Eventually, one Irishman, a banker from Dublin, gave a different answer:

"There's no such thing as the Celtic Tiger," he admitted soberly. "It's a transplanted American Tiger."

Finally, we thought, an explanation that made sense. It wasn't that suddenly Ireland had created new industries. Ireland wasn't manufacturing any new products or providing any new services. What they had managed to do, by offering tax breaks and other incentives, was to entice foreign industries, mostly American at first, to migrate to Ireland. These transplanted industries (call centers, computer manufacturing plants) injected not only investment capital but also population into a country best known for exporting those things. Before this time and throughout the country's history, its best and brightest had gone elsewhere in search of opportunity. They, like young Denis today, recognized that their own country was no place for the ambitious.

However, when the Ireland Development Authority (IDA) succeeded, starting in the early 1990s, in attracting foreign businesses and investors to Irish shores, they reversed this trend. Foreign investor capital flowed across the green isle triggering an age of growth. The entrepreneurs, the executives, and the workforces who answered the IDA's call had something that this country had never known before—disposable income. For the first time in Ireland's history, young Irish lads and lasses could afford to move out of their parents' homes before they got married and certainly after. The building boom that followed was reminiscent of the Baby Boom in the United States following World War II. Euphoria took hold. The Irish were making money, spending money, investing money, having babies, and more than anything else, it seemed, building houses. All those new families needed places to live, after all.

Over the seven years we were residents of the Emerald Isle, this run continued. We watched year after year as the Irish continued to buy and sell land and houses, one to another, and each year we predicted the peak. Surely, this year would be the one when this Irish property bubble would burst. This growth couldn't continue. Nothing real was behind it. But it did continue, even for a couple of years after we took our leave of this market. By the time we moved from Ireland to France, Dublin property prices exceeded those of Paris on a per-square-meter basis. How could that be?

Moving from Waterford to Paris, we expected our cost of living to increase. We'd watched costs in Ireland rise throughout the seven years we'd been living there. Costs for everything from groceries to doctor's visits and from taxi rides to office staff (we were running a business) had gone up 100 percent and more during our time as Irish residents. Still, we assumed, life in Paris would be costlier. Paris is . . . Paris. What we found, though, was that upon living in Paris, our overall cost of living was reduced by about 20 percent compared with what it had been in Waterford. Again, how could that be, we wondered.

The rapid rates of inflation that Ireland experienced throughout the Celtic Tiger era were a big contributor to the end of the Celtic Tiger era. The foreign businesses that opened offices and invested in plants in Ireland to take advantage of IDA incentives were also counting on low costs of labor and of doing business. When those things moved from cheap to expensive, the foreign businesses moved on (to Eastern Europe, for example), taking their transplanted Tiger boom with them.

Today, the Irish economy, banking industry, and property market have collapsed. The Irish construction industry, once responsible for feeding the Celtic Tiger, is all but insolvent. Real estate across the country is on offer for as little as 50 percent, 60 percent, and less of what it sold for pre-2008, and prices continue down. The market isn't stable enough to accept all the foreclosed real estate on the books, so the government and the banks are holding many properties to the side, especially in small, localized markets, where the number of foreclosures as a percentage of the market overall could be crushing.

One of the biggest challenges facing both buyers and sellers considering the Irish real estate market today is that prices are all over the place. The Irish have been so far removed from reality for the past decade and a half that they have no idea what any piece of property is worth. The post–Celtic Tiger Irish property market is more Latin American than European. In a market like this one, you can't pay attention to list prices, and you shouldn't be afraid to offer half what's being asked. Again, no one has any idea what any piece of property is "worth" in Ireland today, meaning it's worth what a ready buyer with cash in his pocket is willing to pay.

Is it time to buy? This market fooled me for so long, continuing to appreciate beyond all reason and for no reason for years, with me all the while continually predicting its collapse, so I'm reluctant to try to pin it down now. That said, if you've ever dreamt of a home of your own on the Emerald Isle, I'd have to say that, yes, right now could be the best time in your lifetime to go shopping for it.

When you do, I'd hold any investment agenda to the side. Don't expect capital appreciation in the next five years at least; probably values in this country won't rebound even over the coming decade. However, that needn't be the point and shouldn't interfere with any retirement or lifestyle agenda.

Ireland holds out the promise of a peaceful, tranquil retirement amid landscapes and seascapes that qualify as among the world's most glorious. This country has long been a top retirement choice, as it is a beautiful, welcoming, peaceful nation of friendly, hospitable folks who speak English and who have a long-standing affinity with the United States. For decades, the retirement daydream of many Americans has been a whitewashed, thatched-roof cottage on the Emerald Isle. In the course of but two decades, Ireland has seen unprecedented boom and dramatic bust. Through the wild up and down, she has retained her heart. Irish retirement living is as appealing and charming an idea as it ever was, and today it's also, once again, affordable.

One good way to access some of this country's best current bargains is at auction. Ireland is one place where property continues to trade hands at auction, and, in this post–Celtic Tiger climate, banks are using auctions as a way to clear foreclosed inventory from their books. You can find out more about upcoming distressed property auctions at http://www.allsop.co.uk /283/irish-auctions. Focus on the main cities of Dublin, Galway, and Cork. Some of the smaller cities, such as Wexford and Waterford, might offer opportunities that make sense as well, but unless you personally want to be based in one of those small towns, you are better off sticking with higher population areas. Depressed and falling prices alongside escalating rents are pushing rental yields beyond the anemic 2 percent and lower rates you could expect during the boom days. In Dublin at the moment, annual return from rental income can amount to 7 percent and more.

Also note that, as of this writing, Ireland is contemplating a property tax. My young friend Denis thinks it's a done deal. "I think we are beyond the point of contemplating a property tax," he told me. "Dublin's mind is made up. It seems like it's going to happen by 2014. A household charge has been imposed meantime to get us used to the idea. The reality is that Ireland is facing a new property tax." If this is indeed the case and a new tax is implemented, it could help to push property prices down even further.

Crisis Buy 3: Spain—Where Have All the British Gone?

"I moved to Sitges, Catalonia, Spain, in 2001," friend Lucy Culpepper explains. "We rented a four-bedroom house with a community pool and gardens in a beautiful urbanization in walking distance of Mediterranean beaches. A house in the same complex was on the market for about 350,000 euro. The area was stable with a small amount of development going on in the hills behind us.

"By 2006, every available piece of land, including plots that barely clung to the hillside, was being built on. There were more building cranes on the skyline than TV aerials, construction trucks raced about everywhere, and the sound of building crashed around us. Another house in our complex came on the market in mid-2007. It sold for 540,000 euro. By now the town was heaving with real estate offices with multilingual expat real estate agents selling to every European market. *Se vende* signs were everywhere, on both new and secondhand homes of owners trying to make a killing on long-held family properties. By the beginning of 2008, things were looking worrying— there were so many empty new builds, some abandoned. Builders were simply running out of money. The cranes had stopped swinging, and the mood had darkened."

At the beginning of December 2009, one of Spain's biggest banks, Caixa Catalunya, published a report stating that housing prices would not fall any lower. Just a few days later, the property consulting group Aguirre Newman published its report, which predicted: "The residential property market in Spain has not yet reached bottom and could drop another 27 percent in 2010." The Aguirre Newman report went on to explain that property transactions had fallen by around 41 percent in 2009 compared with 2008 and warned that bank valuations continued to overestimate the true value of property in Spain. Aguirre Newman was right. Prices continued down through 2010, 2011, and 2012.

Have we seen the bottom yet? Is it time to buy? Before we attempt to answer that question, let's look at how Spain found itself in this sorry state.

Boom Days on the Med

In 1986, Spain entered the European Union, which led to a rise in living standards and an overhaul of the country's financial markets. Spain received massive farming, fishing, and infrastructure subsidies from the European Union, enabling its transformation from a backwater to a more legitimate economy and, most important, creating jobs. The country recovered quickly from the 1990 worldwide recession, leap-frogging over preexisting technologies, particularly those of the burgeoning cell phone and Internet industries. Spaniards had more available income and more credit, and northern Europeans were becoming increasingly mobile and interested in expat living and second-home ownership on the sunny shores of the Mediterranean.

This led, in the decade from 1997 to 2007, to a massive property boom. By 2007, construction represented 16 percent of GDP and 12 percent of recorded total employment, and, in reality, construction-related employment rates were probably much greater. Huge numbers of construction workers flooded Spain from Eastern Europe and worked off the books. According to Organisation for Economic Cooperation and Development (OECD) figures, between 2000 and 2005, Spain created more than half the new jobs in all of Europe. By 2004, Spain had the highest home ownership uptake and the lowest public housing rate in the Western world.

Along with the building boom came a pricing boom. In the decade from 1997 to 2007, Spain's national house price average increased by 197 percent. Along the Mediterranean coastline, where northern Europeans were flocking by airplane loads, prices rose by 250 percent. Huge numbers of housing developments sprang up in southern Spain. Most followed planning laws, but many did not.

Spain's property bubble grew and grew until the inevitable happened and it burst. When the worldwide crisis hit, credit dried up overnight, and the planeloads of northern Europeans disappeared. Developers went from selling inventory faster than they could deliver it to drowning in debt within months.

Epic Bust

Why did the global crisis hit Spain so fast and so hard? The answer is simple overbuilding on a massive scale. Developers believed that the planeloads of eager buyers were endless, and they were building to supply that perceived potential. In 2006 alone, 800,000 homes were built in Spain, more than in France, Germany, and Italy combined. A large percentage of property owners who bought during the boom years were second-home or buy-to-let investors; they didn't have the stomach to hold on to their properties when they saw prices falling. Many were British owners who had remortgaged a UK property to pay for a Spanish one. With rising interest rates in the United Kingdom, it became impossible for these British owners to hold on to their homes on the *costas*. Some sold, some lost their homes, and the situation certainly deterred other Brits from shopping.

Part of the problem, too, was that because Spain was part of the eurozone, it could not set interest rates to suit its economy. Eurozone interest rates were being set with Germany in mind, and Germany was at the opposite end of a 10-year business cycle compared to Spain. The low interest rates fueled borrowing in Spain (both by businesses and individuals) during the boom days, and that heavy borrowing had encouraged excessively loose lending conditions. During this time, Spaniards also became hard-hitting credit card users, building up high levels of personal debt, a completely new phenomenon in a country where people previously had a cautious better-to-stick-it-under-the-mattress perspective when it came to deciding what to do with their money.

As in most of Europe, the most popular mortgage in Spain throughout the boom buying period was variable rate. This wasn't a problem when rates were falling, as they did for a long time. In 1991, the interest rate in this country was 17 percent. By 1995, it was 10 to 12 percent. By 2004, it was less than 3.5 percent. Rates fell to an historic low of 1 percent in 2009 and have crept up steadily since, to just above 3 percent as of this writing. Ninety-six percent of mortgage holders in Spain are affected by this rising rate of interest, with the prospect of worse to come.

As a result, the scene on the ground along the coast of Spain today is near-desolation and near-desperation. Massive numbers of properties are available at hugely discounted prices. The average price of real estate in this country has fallen by well more than 50 percent since 2006. In June 2006, the average per-square-meter cost to buy an apartment in Spain was 3,500 euro; in June 2012, it was 1,633 euro. Spanish banks hold approximately 1 billion euro worth of inventory that they are desperate to get rid of, meaning there are massive savings to be had on the purchase of repossessed property, most of which never made it to market. Entire developments near the sea lie empty; the builder and/or the developer went bust. Google "repossessed Spanish bank property," and you'll get hundreds of thousands of matches. The list prices on most websites are whimsy; vendors know they're not going to get what they're asking.

The biggest bargains (and usually best locations) are repossessed new builds. Santander's property site, Altamira, has a two-bedroom apartment in a new development in Estepona for 92,299 euro. ServiHabitat, the property arm of La Caixa, is asking buyers to make offers on their site. At a recent property exhibition in London, a company offered all-inclusive, three-day viewing tours of property on the Costa Blanca and Costa del Sol for 99 pounds ($160). That included flight from the United Kingdom, hotel, and food. Another exhibitor, Property Repossessions Spain, focuses on the Murcia region of Andalusia (where Paramount Pictures is developing a theme park). They list deeply discounted villas, apartments, and condos, most of which have never been lived in, are fully furnished, and include every amenity. A two-bedroom, two-bathroom apartment in Pueblo Salinas, Vera, just a 10-minute walk to the beach, is reduced from 294,000 euro to 133,000 euro. A 100 percent, low-rate mortgage is available with payments of 270 euro per month. At Mar Menor, a two-bedroom, one-bathroom furnished apartment in a luxury apartment block with swimming pools that is only 400 meters from a sandy beach is reduced from 195,000 euro to 85,000 euro. It's close to golf courses and is within 35 minutes of an international airport and the coming Paramount theme park. You could move in with a 5,000-euro down payment based on a 100 percent mortgage and monthly payments of 310 euro.

The Spanish government has changed its property rental laws, making them more pro-landlord, especially for foreign landlords. The hope is that this will help to inspire foreign buyers to consider returning to this currently all-but-abandoned marketplace. The new tax relief plan allows landlords to keep 100 percent of the rental income generated from a rental investment.

Is it time to buy? Certainly, you'll want to do your due diligence. Mostly empty developments and apartment buildings beg questions about home-owner association (HOA) fees and building or development maintenance. That aside, if you like the Spanish coast and want to own there simply because you want to own there, not because you think you might make money owning there, then, yes, this is the time to buy. My main recommendation would be to avoid areas awash in cookie-cutter condos. Look for more unique properties with charm and intrinsic value. These will hold value better in the long term. As in any coastal market, front line to the sea is always best.

Crisis Buy 4: Nicaragua— Never Mind Ortega

"Forget about the Sandinistas. They're obsolete."

That was Violeta Chamorro's advice in September 1989, when asked about her chances for defeating the Sandinistas in Nicaragua's first presidential election after the civil war. To the surprise of sitting President Daniel Ortega and all Nicaragua, Mrs. Chamorro won that election in

February 1990. The Sandinista Ortega stepped down graciously, and Doña Violeta began the work of rebuilding her country.

I visited Nicaragua for the first time three years later. Managua, thanks to the earthquake of 1972, the revolution, and the civil war, was a near disaster zone. No reason at the time to stick around and this is only slightly less true today. Gringos like me, then and now, migrated instead slightly west and south, to the Pacific coast, where, by the early 1990s, speculators had already begun snatching up stretches of this country's primo beachfront, and inland, to the colonial city of Granada.

Visiting Granada for the first time during that initial scouting trip in 1993, I found a single hotel, the Alhambra, recognizable (still today) by its long, breezy porch overlooking the city's central square. A rocking chair in front of the Alhambra is the best perch in this city. Back in the early and mid-1990s, the hotel itself was a much less appealing place to spend time, with rusty fixtures in the leaky bathrooms and cockroaches under the creaky cot beds. The Alhambra has since been renovated, along with much of the rest of Granada.

Although both Granada and Nicaragua historically have been and can still be short on amenities, they have always been long on heart. When I discovered Nicaragua, the country was pulling itself up by the bootstraps. In the towns and traveling along the dirt roads back then, you saw men and boys in olive green military garb, sometimes carrying weapons. They seemed intimidating, until you stopped to speak with them. They talked openly of their desire for peace. These Nicaraguans were tired of fighting, worn out by decades of watching their once-prosperous little country dissolve into chaos.

In the years that followed, the transformation was remarkable. The gringos kept coming and even began settling in. Speculation along the Nicaraguan Pacific Riviera went into overdrive. Sleepy Granada became a tourist hub, so crowded you'd sometimes have to wait your turn for a rocking chair on the porch of the Alhambra. Doña Violeta, it seemed, had been right. The Sandinistas had become obsolete, just like the political model they'd sought to follow, replaced, it appeared for some time, by property investors, foreign retirees, and adventure-entrepreneurs. Indeed, through 2006, Nicaragua was on the fast track to a bigger, brighter future.

That is not to say that the Sandinistas—the party or the people—had disappeared. Indeed, the most famous Sandinista of all, Daniel Ortega, once again, is president. How did that happen? You'd have to ask the Nicaraguans. They reelected him, putting him back in office in 2007. As a result, all those investors, retirees, and entrepreneurs who had tied their dreams to Nicaragua's post-Sandinista future panicked. The panic deepened when, in 2011, Ortega adjusted things so that he could run for a consecutive term as president, something that had previously been prohibited in the country's constitution. Ortega ran again and was reelected. Once more, you'd have to talk to the Nicaraguans to understand the thinking behind this—it's a mystery.

In the meantime, in 2008–2009, U.S. and world real estate markets began to tumble, compounding investor panic further and creating a perfect storm of negative influences that succeeded in nearly annihilating Nicaragua's property market. All of Central America (with the notable exception of Panama) has been hit hard by the global recession, but Nicaragua has been hit harder than its neighbors. Historically, the majority of foreign property buyers in this country have come from the United States and Canada. Most of these buyers leveraged property assets back home to find the money to acquire new Nicaraguan assets. That hasn't been a realistic option for some time now, meaning that Nicaragua's buying pool has evaporated.

I don't see this changing in the short term, despite what some Nicaraguan developers you might speak with might argue, meaning that I don't see Nicaragua as a place to buy for quick growth. On the other hand, the retiree willing to take a longer-term view should be looking at Nicaragua right now. This is a market close to the bottom of its crisis cycle. Thinking long haul and putting this opportunity into perspective, Nicaragua boasts something that will always be in demand: Pacific coastal real estate reminiscent of the best of southern California. Right now, values along this country's long and dramatically beautiful Pacific coastline are down 40 and 50 percent from their peaks, and developers are uncharacteristically open to offers. It's possible to buy in a full-amenity development for as little as $30,000, sometimes even with developer financing. In Granada, Nicaragua's other key expat and investor market, it's possible today to buy one of the small Spanish colonial houses the city is famous for as little as $40,000 or $50,000.

Politics have too long distracted people from recognizing what Nicaragua has to offer. Take Doña Violeta's advice and forget about Ortega and the Sandinistas. Two and a half decades ago, they tried to make a new Nicaragua. Fortunately for you and me, the old Nicaragua, the largest but least-visited nation in Central America, lives on. This Nicaragua is a beautiful country with loads of sunshine and two long coasts, one of white sand, one with crashing surf. It is a land of lakes and volcanoes, of cloud forests and tropical jungles, of cattle ranches and Spanish colonial cities (including two of the oldest cities in the Americas, Granada and León, both classic colonial towns with shady plazas and centuries-old Spanish colonial architectural gems), of rare orchids and white-faced capuchin monkeys, and, most recently, of a new-and-improved, foreign retiree residency program.

Nicaragua is a land of pirates, martyrs, heroes, warriors, and poets, fighting each in his way for what he believes. Colonial León is at the heart of many of the country's struggles, historically its quixotic center. León is proud to be known as the place where the last of the Somoza dynasty finally ran out of bullets, bombs, and power in 1979. The red-and-black flag of the FSLN (Sandinista National Liberation Front) waves proudly over the monuments and the city hall, where, still, vendors hawk souvenirs of those valiant, bloody times.

Perhaps, though, what struck me most during my first visit to Nicaragua years ago and what has continued to draw me back to this country all these years since is the spirit of the Nicaraguan people. On my first visit, I met a young Nicaraguan man, 20 or 22 years old. "When I was very small," he told me one afternoon, "the soldiers came for my family. It was the middle of the night. We were all asleep inside. The soldiers were in a pickup truck. They stopped out front and came to the door. They woke us all up and told us that our house was needed for the revolution. In the name of the revolution, they told us, we had to get out.

"We all climbed into the back of their pickup truck, and the soldiers drove us into the mountains. They left us there, my whole family. We had nothing with us. But my father made us a place to live . . . and we survived.

"That is our past," the young man told me in perfect English. "But it is not our future."

This young man, like many others in Nicaragua, had taught himself to speak English by watching American television ("mostly MTV," I remember him saying).

Thinking practically, Nicaragua's big advantage is its cost of living, which is among the lowest you'll find anywhere in the world that you might actually want to live. The Ortega Factor has frightened off many would-be retirees and expats looking for a budget destination, but not all. Both retirees and tourists in search of low-cost adventure continue to make their way to this country, which offers an affordable lifestyle bundled with the chance to start over.

A final practical note: Nicaragua uses the cordoba (which, unlike most other currencies these days, has been falling faster than the U.S. dollar, meaning that, although the U.S. expat's buying power has been steadily reduced worldwide, in Nicaragua, it continues to increase). Note, as well, however, that real estate in this country is priced and trades in U.S. dollars.

6 Buy for the Income

A ny global real estate investment portfolio should include at least one rental property. A rental investment won't make you rich, but it can provide solid, reliable returns. Your target for a net yield from a rental property investment should be 5 to 8 percent net per year. This is a reasonable expectation in a normal market, and, in the current investment climate, it's nothing to sneeze at. Identify a market where some distortion (because of undersupply, greater than historically typical demand, seriously undervalued purchase prices, or rising rents) is at work, and you can do better.

How do you get started building a portfolio of rental investments? Where should you be looking now to expand an existing portfolio? The surest bet is to target markets with proven tourist track records, places that attract visitors even when times are tough. Paris is the best example.

Second, consider inventory supply and demand. The Costa del Sol, for example, is ridiculously oversupplied.

Third, as with any real estate investment overseas, think through your exit strategy from the start. Even if your intention is to hold the rental long term, understand who your eventual buyer might be. You won't likely hold forever, and, regardless of your intended timeline until exit, it's a good idea to have an idea when going into any investment of whom you might sell to when you're ready to cash out.

The key consideration, though, when looking to buy to let overseas—and more important, I would argue, than what you buy—is the system for managing what you buy. You can act as your own rental manager, but I don't advise it. If you're not residing physically in the same place as the rental unit, I say definitely don't do it. I've had 15 years of investor-landlord experience in more than a dozen countries. This isn't something you want to take on yourself, unless you're prepared to make it your full-time occupation. Rather, you want to engage someone who knows the market, who has marketing infrastructure in place, who has developed a client list you can leverage, and who can show you proven management systems (for reservations, inventory control, reporting, etc.).

My first apartment investment in Paris rented extraordinarily well the first year. However, the French rental manager spoke no English and was perpetually late with reporting. So I switched to another manager, an American. Yes, he spoke English, but he, too, was perpetually late with reporting. More to the point, he achieved less than half the occupancy I'd enjoyed the year before, even though the market was stronger and tourism was up.

This is why I say that, when you make a rental investment, you're choosing, first, a market; next, a rental manager; and, finally, a property. Before you make a particular purchase decision, seek advice from the rental management agency you're planning to work with. What's more rentable? Two bedrooms or one? What matters most to would-be renters? Location, of course, but other, less obvious things can be critical. In Paris, you'll struggle to make a decent return off a fifth-floor rental in an apartment building with no elevator.

Specifically, what expertise are you looking for in a rental manager? The best ones we've hired have impressed us with their discriminating judgment. One, in Paris, made a point of telling us, with a voice of long experience, to whom she would not rent: "We won't rent to such-and-such people, because they throw wild parties," "We won't rent to so-and-so people, because they don't respect other people's property," and so on. In some contexts, her positions might be termed discrimination. We saw them as risk management, and managing risk is a critical part of being a long-distance landlord for overseas rental investment properties, because there are so many ways things can go wrong. You need systems to manage bookings, renter comings and goings, payments, expenses, cleaning, inventory, repairs, maintenance, renter complaints, keys, and breakage. Plus, you need a system for generating reservations. Where will you advertise? How will you market? That's perhaps the most important thing a good management company brings to the table—a developed marketing and reservations system. In addition, a good management company will:

- Be flexible enough to accommodate reservation changes and to fill the gaps. Say you've got someone in your place for two weeks and then someone arriving three days after Renter #1 departs for another two-week stay. A good management agency (in an active market) will fill a couple of those gap nights.
- Meet and greet every renter. A representative from the management company should meet each renter, deliver the keys, explain systems (how the DVD player works, the trick to using the dishwasher, where to find the air-conditioning controls), suggest restaurants and services in the area, answer questions, and so on. Some of these things should also be explained in full in a renter's manual, conspicuously displayed in the property.
- Perform a post-renter check to look for damages, verify inventory, and confirm cleaning.
- Keep a detailed and current inventory of everything in the unit from wine glasses to pillowcases.
- Contact you immediately if anything is damaged or broken. I owned a rental apartment in Buenos Aires a few years ago. Our rental manager there neglected to inform me for two months of a leak in the master bedroom. In fact, she never did inform me. I got in touch with her when I noticed in her reports that the place hadn't been rented for weeks. Nada. "*Que pasa*?" I e-mailed to ask her. "Oh, well, I can't rent the place with all that water damage in the bedroom . . ."
- Solicit estimates for necessary repairs, oversee the repairs, and update you in real time as to the associated costs.
- Send you (by e-mail) regular reports (say, monthly) on occupancy, nightly rental rates, expenses, fees, taxes, and (with luck) profits.
- Respond to your e-mails. You'd be surprised how many times this final point becomes the most challenging.

One agency I worked with in Paris regularly left renters standing alone and confused outside the front door to the apartment building waiting for someone to show up with the key to let them inside. Another agency I worked with in Paris never thought to keep an inventory of apartment contents. I'd visit now and then to check on things to discover that there was a single drinking glass in the cabinet or but two lonely forks in the cutlery drawer.

It's the exceptional agency anywhere that remembers to factor in all related expenses, fees, taxes, and so on, in projections and even in reporting. In Paris, for example, don't forget the building fee (it's called the *syndic* fee) or the local property taxes that you, the owner, are liable for (called the *taxe d'habitation* and the *taxe fonciere*). And don't forget to plan for the things that can't be planned for—leaks in the bedroom ceiling, exploding water heaters, lost keys (it costs $150-plus each to have a key made in France), and so on.

How do you find a good rental manager? Ask for references from other landlords who've been invested in the market for some time. Interview at least two. Go with a professional. By this, I mean someone who is focused full-time and working to make money. I've made the mistake of engaging folks who managed apartment rentals on the side, as a hobby, or as a part-time occupation in retirement. I will not make that mistake again. You want someone with an established infrastructure (for advertising, taking reservations if you're renting short term, negotiating contracts if you're renting long term, reporting, etc.); existing support (for meeting tenants upon arrival with the keys, responding to tenants' cries for help to turn up the heat in the middle of the night, and managing things like inventory in the case of a furnished rental); and a proven track record (for bringing in renters, keeping track of cash flow, and making sure that the local tax and utility bills are paid on time). You don't want to work with the friend of a friend who has been managing his own apartment rental for a couple of years and who is now looking to expand to manage others' investments as well.

In most markets, things such as commission structure and percentage and what's included for that fee are standardized, although you will want to confirm and clarify this in every case.

Finally, note that property management and rental management can be two different things. Some rental managers are also willing and able to act as property managers but charge an additional fee. Your rental manager is responsible for keeping your rental rented. You're paying this manager for his or her marketing infrastructure and ability to bring you tenants. Your property manager is responsible for managing and maintaining the rental property itself. You're paying that manager to take care of cleaning, manage repairs, keep a property inventory, replace supplies and broken/damaged items, and to pay associated local bills and expenses (electric bill, phone bill, annual tax bill, etc.). The combined costs of property and rental management vary from 20 to 40 percent of rental income, depending on the market.

Short Term versus Long Term

A few years ago, on a visit to Paris to check on our apartment there, I sat down with our rental manager, Linda, one afternoon.

"Every one of my apartments is rented," she told me. "In fact, I need more inventory."

Yet, at the time, our apartment had been vacant since our tenant of one year had vacated a few months earlier. Three months without cash flow later, I was growing concerned.

"If all of your apartments are rented, and you could fill more if you had them," I couldn't help but wonder aloud with Linda that afternoon, "why is ours sitting vacant?"

"But you said you wanted long-term rentals only," Linda replied. "We will find one, I'm certain. It will just take more time."

"But if we allowed short-term renters?" I asked.

"Oh, I'd have someone in here within two weeks. If you were open to short-term clients, you could have been fully occupied these past three months, just like all my other apartments."

One of the advantages of real estate investing overseas in general and of rental investments overseas in particular is that, when an asset isn't returning according to expectations, you can adjust the asset. Bought a house in a resort region where there's a lot of competition for rentals? Improve your chances of attracting would-be renters' attention by adding a swimming pool. Invested in an apartment in a place without zoning restrictions and having trouble finding tenants? Try advertising your asset as commercial rather than residential. Struggling to fill your long-term rental in Paris? Offer it on the short-term market.

There are pluses and minuses for both long and short term. For me, the biggest short-term minus is the wear and tear it can mean on the property. Holiday-makers coming and going week after week take less care and cause more damage than a retired couple settled in for a couple of years. Each new renter must learn how to use the dishwasher, the washing machine, and the heating system. In the process, breakage is unavoidable. Tourists staying in an apartment for a week or two are not going to replace a glass or a dish when they break one, but someone living in the place for a year eventually has no choice. With short-term tenants, keys get lost, and knickknacks disappear. You must accept all this from the get-go.

Long term comes with a downside, too. If your place is rented 100 percent of the time, you can never use it yourself. In addition, in most markets, long term typically means reduced net return.

Sizing Up a Rental Investment

Your return from any rental investment overseas (that is, the amount of cash flow you're able to generate and how much of it is left over after all associated costs have been covered) depends first and foremost on the market. Are there renters enough to go around? Consider both the supply of rentals and the existing or anticipated demand. You may need to break things down, as different rental markets may exist in parallel—one for tourists and another for executives on extended-stay contracts, for example. A family of holiday-makers is looking for a different kind of rental property than a banker from Japan on assignment, even if each is shopping for a rental in the same area of the same city.

The second key to a good rental return, as I've discussed, is the rental/property manager. A good manager can translate to a good return from a decent rental in a decent market. A bad manager can mean no return even from a great rental in a booming market. The third variable affecting return is the type of rental you choose to buy and what you do with it. In most markets, a one-bedroom property makes most sense, but there are exceptions. In Paris, for example, one-bedroom rentals are a glut on the market. Two-bedroom rentals are in shorter supply, meaning that, if you can afford it, a two-bedroom rental can make more sense and yield a greater return.

In a beach market, a beachfront unit is key. People are coming for the sand and the sea. Front-line units will always enjoy better occupancy. In a city high-rise market, you want a building with an elevator, a doorman, security, competitive building amenities (in Panama City, for example, lots of new inventory is coming online and renters are choosing based on building amenities as much as any other factor; the newest buildings have the best amenities), parking, and day-to-day services (grocery store, newsstand, restaurants, dry cleaners, etc.) within walking distance.

Your return is also affected by whether you choose to put your place on the short- or the long-term market. To make this decision, you must understand the current dynamics of the marketplace. Who comprises the biggest potential tenant population? Visiting businesspeople (short term)? Business executives placed in the country on extended contracts (long term)? Tourists (short term)? Retirees (long term)? When making this determination, also consider the local tenant laws. In some jurisdictions, a long-term tenant can be all but impossible to displace if he decides he doesn't want to move on. In France, for example, you won't be able to evict a tenant (no matter how many months in arrears he is with the rent) in winter. The French say that you can't put someone out on the street in the cold.

Finally, you must decide whether to rent furnished or not. If you intend to rent short term, you should definitely furnish your unit. If you'll be renting long term, you may wish to furnish, depending on the market-place. When considering this to-furnish-or-not-to-furnish question, understand what *furnished* and *unfurnished* mean in the local context. In some markets, unfurnished requires blinds or drapes at the windows; in others, it means you don't even have to spring for appliances, lighting fixtures, or a doorbell. If you decide to rent your property furnished, remember to budget for the fixtures, the furniture, and the finishes, and to take those costs into account when projecting and figuring your net return on investment.

You're Also Buying the Building

My husband, Lief, has recently been elected to the board of directors for the owners association of a building in Panama City, where we own a rental investment property. The experience is giving us insights into what goes into maintaining a 27-story building. Every owner has his pet peeves and grievances. Lief and his fellow board members listen to them all, while spending a significant number of hours each week trying to keep the building functioning, maintained, and constantly improving.

This speaks to another thing to remember when shopping for a rental investment unit anywhere in the world—in addition to the apartment, you're also buying the building where it's located.

I know of a building in Panama City that has no working elevator. A recent advertisement for an apartment for sale on the fourteenth floor of this building tried to make the best of the situation. It read: "No need for a gym membership when you live here." The price was attractive and reflected the lack of elevator access. The problem is that, eventually, the broken elevator will have to be replaced. This will trigger a special assessment on all building owners. This isn't uncommon. If the cash flow from regular monthly building fees isn't enough to cover both the costs of operating the building and of required maintenance and necessary improvements, well, the money has to come from somewhere.

Or not. And this is the risk. If owners aren't organized and working together, the building and your investment suffer. It won't be possible to get the consensus needed to execute special capital calls, to increase the amount of the monthly building fees, or to carry out big-ticket repairs or improvements. The bottom line result is that the public areas and amenities in the building will deteriorate.

When trying to identify a rental investment, therefore, shop not only location, unit, and price per square meter but also building and building management. Ask about the building association and to see the related documents, including minutes from recent association meetings, financial statements for the building fund, and details of building improvements planned or being considered. Years ago, shopping for our first rental apartment investment in Paris, a friend made a recommendation that I probably didn't appreciate enough at the time. "Try to find out if any big improvements are planned for the building within the next year or two," he told me. "Are they going to add an elevator? Clean the building façade? Relay the cobblestones in the courtyard? Fix a leaking roof?"

Why? Because these are extraordinary expenses that will have to be paid for by a capital call on all owners. To avoid surprises in your first years as an owner, try to find out what kinds of works are being discussed. In France, the *syndic,* or building management association, is a legal entity with a lot of teeth. If your *syndic* tells you that you have to pony up an additional 2,000, 5,000, or even 10,000 euro in a year to cover repairs or improvements to the building, you have no choice but to comply. Well, you can choose not to comply, but the consequences are severe.

In Panama, on the other hand, building associations are haphazard and mismanaged. Sometimes they exist in name only. If the owners don't pay their monthly building fees, what are the building managers and other apartment owners going to do? In any given building in Panama City, you have a percentage, sometimes significant, of absentee owners, including foreigners who bought the unit as a speculative or rental investment. They're in the United States, Canada, Germany, Venezuela, or wherever. How is the typical ad hoc and mismanaged management team in Panama going to chase them down for their $200 a month? The effects of this are beginning to become evident in some buildings in Panama's capital. Broken elevators, faulty plumbing, ill-maintained swimming pools, unkempt social areas . . .

What's your rental apartment worth when the building where it's located is falling down around it? What's your rental return going to be long term?

How to Project Your Cash Flow

Rental properties come in different types: long-term rentals, short-term rentals, condo-hotel units, leasebacks, and even farmland. Generally speaking, your net return on investment works out more or less the same across the board, in the range, as I've suggested, of 5 to 8 percent per year over the long term. However, projecting your true net return can be complicated, as the expenses of owning, maintaining, and renting vary market by market and property type by property type. This is why many in the business of trying to sell you on a particular rental investment opportunity will speak in terms of gross yields. Don't make this mistake. Drill down to a net figure.

The rule of thumb for long-term rentals in the United States is 1 percent of the property value per month, or 12 percent gross return per year. However, the net on that gross could be less than 5 percent, depending on your costs. Depending on the state where you're operating, for example, property taxes can take a big bite out of your gross cash flow. By way of comparison, the gross return from a rental I own in Panama City right now is 9 percent. My net in this case is more than 8 percent, thanks to low costs and low property taxes.

Another point when projecting and tracking your yields: Understand the difference between making your calculations on original purchase price versus current value. Rental yields work like bond yields. If the property value goes down and cash flow remains the same, then the yield goes up. And vice versa. Calculating current yields on the purchase price of a piece of property can lead to bad decisions, especially if you've owned the property for a long time or prices have recently spiked.

Returning to my Panama City rental example, the net yield based on purchase price would be more than 13 percent, as I bought the apartment years ago when prices were lower than they are today. That return, though, is misleading. If I sold the property and reinvested the proceeds in another investment, I wouldn't be able to realize the same yield on the greater capital amount.

A colleague in Bali got my attention a few years ago by quoting rental yields of up to 18 percent per year in that market; however, when pushed for details, it turned out that true net yields were running more in the range of 5 to 6 percent. That is, they were typical. References to exceptionally high yields are one of two things—blatantly untrue (once you drill down to true net) or the result of a market distortion creating a window of opportunity that won't last long. A few years ago, for example, you could, in fact, earn double-digit net yields from a beach rental in Punta del Este. After a couple of years, though, the gap between cost of acquisition and annual rental revenues narrowed, and, today, net yields on this part of Uruguay's coast are in the range of what you should more or less expect generally, anywhere in the world—5 to 8 percent.

Top Cash-Flow Markets

If you're a retiree or lifestyle buyer shopping for a piece of property overseas that will generate cash flow when you're not using it yourself, you can direct your search according to your personal agenda. Where do you want to be? Target the country and the city where you want to spend time and then shop for a property with rental potential in that location, taking into account the recommendations and parameters I've outlined.

If you're an investor-buyer interested in expanding your real estate portfolio to include rental property, target markets with track records for rental returns and/or growing rental demand. Paris is the world's most proven rentals market—not that Paris doesn't see down cycles. Since 1965, property values fell twice before the most recent 2008 global property decline. In both cases, prices rebounded within five to eight years, and they are rebounding now in the wake of the 2008 fall. You're not buying in Paris for rapid appreciation, though you can well enjoy appreciation as a long-term property owner. You're buying in Paris for cash flow. Gross rental yields in Paris have been reliably in the range of 10 percent per year and better for a century (which generally nets to 5 to 8 percent).

France is the most visited country in the world. It sees nearly 80 million tourists annually, most of whom spend time in Paris. It's hard to imagine this changing anytime soon. Good times and bad, bull markets and bear, people come to Paris. There aren't enough hotel rooms to hold them all, and some passing through prefer to stay in apartments anyway. Thus, Paris's rental industry is organized and efficient. The investor-buyer can enjoy the best returns on the short-term rental market. The problem is that technically, short-term rentals are illegal in Paris and have been, according to the Code de la Construction et de l'Habitation, since 1978. One great thing about the French is that, although they love their paperwork, they're happy to ignore the rules when it suits them. It seemed to suit everyone to ignore this rule, until current Mayor Delanoe decided that the city's thriving short-term rentals market was making it too difficult for the average working Parisian to afford a place to live. He has issued warnings and imposed fines, with no widespread effect other than to limit, a little, the supply of available short-term rentals (some owners have switched to long term only or have taken their apartments off the market altogether), which, in turn, has increased rates.

One important factor in favor of Paris as a rental investment market is that it's one place where it's possible for foreigners to borrow locally for the purchase of real estate.

Other markets I like right now for rental return include Medellín, Colombia; Panama City, Panama (if you're able to buy for a reasonable price); Puerto Vallarta, Mexico; Santiago, Chile; Punta del Este, Uruguay; Cebu, the Philippines; Kuala Lumpur, Malaysia; and Budapest, Hungary.

7 Buy Growth

Overseas property markets move through phases. Each phase attracts different kinds of buyers and different kinds of end users and presents different levels of opportunity, as follows:

Phase I. During this very early, predevelopment stage, a market attracts adventure seekers, backpackers, experienced world travelers, and men seeking women (think Asia and, closer to home, Colombia, for example). During this phase, real estate prices are low and unmoving. To buy, you must penetrate to the local market, because no nonlocal market exists, and you must either have a strong tolerance for risk or just want to own something in the place because you like spending time there.

Phase II. If a place has merit and value, eventually word-of-mouth and personal referrals begin to drive traffic to it. During this still predevelopment stage, a market sees its first more mature couples, foreign retirees, virtual employees and entrepreneurs, early commercial and business inquiries, and speculators. A nonlocal market emerges, and values begin to appreciate, slowly.

Phase III. When a market establishes a reputation for value and merit, speculators give way to investors and backpackers are overtaken by retirees and expat entrepreneurs. Institutional investors begin to move in, the second-tier (nonlocal) market becomes more sophisticated and more competitive, and second-home buyers begin shopping. It is during this phase that a market sees its highest rates of appreciation.

Phase IV. An established market with expanding pools of buyers and end users and dramatic levels of appreciation draws wider interest. The international press begins coverage, fueling buying in all segments. Institutional and commercial buyers move in and move the market further. Rapid increases of real estate values continue.

Phase V. This is the Disney World phase, recognizable by full-scale international development and investment and big influxes of foreign expats, retirees, and second-home owners. Resorts are built, the major hotels move in, and value appreciation continues for a while before topping out.

If you can identify a market in any stage of Phase III or in the early stages of Phase IV, you can buy almost anything in that location and do well. A market in these growth stages of development offers an abundance of opportunity. In the golden era of global property investing (the decade leading up to 2008), many markets could be described as offering an abundance of opportunity. In the current climate, this idea is all but obsolete, with notable exceptions.

Growth Buy 1: Panama—Gunning for First World Status

Panama's real gross domestic product (GDP) growth rates averaged 8.1 percent between 2004 and 2009, and Panama even managed to grow 2.4 percent in 2009 when economies of most of the rest of the world were shrinking. Growth in 2010 rebounded to 7.5 percent and continued at a rate of 10.5 percent for 2011. GDP for 2012 is projected at better than 11 percent.

One of the main drivers behind this growth has been foreign direct investment. Inflows reached $1.7 billion in 2009 and $3 billion in 2011, a sizable bet by foreign companies on the future of this small country. Big companies from around the world taking advantage of Panama's open-door policies and incentive programs include Maersk Line, Halliburton, Procter & Gamble (P&G), Dell, Caterpillar, and Sinopec, among a total of 68 thus far.

Thanks to all this growth, the country's unemployment rate has dropped significantly, from between 8 percent and 12 percent (depending on which set of numbers you use) to around 4 percent today.

In a series of announcements made March through June 2010, the three leading U.S.-based credit rating agencies improved their ratings for Panama. Then, in 2011, all three agencies upgraded their ratings for Panama once more. Panama has joined a select group of countries in the region with investment-grade status.

Tourism was up 12 percent in 2010 over 2009 (up 20 percent from Spain alone) and up another 10 percent in 2011.

By almost any metric you want to measure it, Panama's current economic state is enviable.

Martinelli's Five-Year Plan

What's going on? Why is this market expanding so rapidly and so reliably while many others worldwide are in recession and worse? Why have dozens of major international companies chosen to establish headquarters here? Why are kids not only from elsewhere in the region but also from the United States, the Emerald Isle, and other farther-flung down markets seeking out the Hub of the Americas when it comes time to find gainful employment? Why does Panama offer such an abundance of opportunity right now?

You could say that it's because of the infrastructure. It's better here in Panama than anywhere else in Central America. Transportation, telecommunications, and banking all exist at a higher level and work on a more reliable basis than anywhere else in this part of the world. But that's a superficial explanation.

The real question becomes why is the infrastructure better in Panama? It has a lot to do with the extended U.S. presence over the past century. However, again, that's only a partial explanation. The reason why Panama's infrastructure is continually expanding and improving is because of current President Ricardo Martinelli's Five-Year Plan. In this part of the world, having a plan isn't such a big deal. Everybody down here in the lands of bananas and *mañanas* has a plan. Martinelli's Five-Year Plan is notable because Martinelli is actually implementing it.

Immediately upon taking office, President Martinelli published his 122-page plan (drafted with the help of McKinsey & Company) in English and then he set about making it happen. Martinelli's Five-Year Plan includes things such as building a new 13.7-kilometer-long metro across the capital; developing a new government city where 200 government offices will be consolidated, saving the country millions of dollars a year in rent; the cleanup of the Bay of Panama (a long time coming and really necessary); and the development of Panama Pacífico, a new city across the Bridge of the Americas, where business development is being further encouraged by tax breaks and other perks (and where many of those international companies I mentioned earlier are choosing to establish headquarters).

Martinelli's Five-Year Plan amounts to a total investment of about $4 billion. Where does Martinelli think this little country is going to get all that money? The Panama Canal. In the 10-plus years since ownership of the Canal changed hands from the United States to Panama, the Panamanians have generated more than $4.5 billion in surplus Canal revenues. Panama has increased annual tonnage figures and prices, while decreasing Canal transit time from 33 to 23 hours. The world's big shipping outfits are happy to pay more to get where they're going quicker. Now the Panamanians are in the process of expanding the Canal, pushing ahead in typically aggressive Panamanian style with a $5.25 billion expansion of their biggest asset.

The Trouble with Buying in Panama

That's why Panama offers an abundance of opportunity for the would-be property buyer. The challenge can be taking advantage of it. I've been paying attention to Panama's property markets for more than a dozen years, I made my first investment in this country eight years ago, and I've been living full-time in Panama City for almost five. Here's what I can tell you: This is one crazy place to shop for real estate. All the usual emerging market caveats and frustrations apply. There's no multiple listing service, no way to establish comps, and no way to know how much any piece of property should cost. Net pricing is not uncommon, and the history of ownership can't be taken for granted. Two markets exist, and, if you operate in the gringo market only, you'll pay more than you should.

In addition, Panama is an emerging market in a boom phase. This makes it even harder to understand what you should pay for whatever you decide you want to buy. Here's what you shouldn't pay: the asking price. In some cases, the price on the listing sheet or quoted by the agent is a starting point, and in other cases, it's irrelevant. As one agent admitted during a recent property search in Panama City: "This is Panama, you understand. Everything is negotiable."

Part of the problem is that many (maybe all) sellers in Panama are in denial. Their real estate assets enjoyed notable appreciation from 2005 to

2008. Then world markets, including the one in Panama, shifted. In some countries, as we've discussed, the shifts were dramatic and even fatal. In Panama, the shift was more subtle. Still, there was a shift. After three to five years of aggressive growth, localized markets across this country softened and stalled. In Panama City, prices fell by about 20 percent between 2008 and 2010/2011. It's harder to get a read on prices outside the capital, but they fell, too. Buyers had the upper hand and sellers across the country were open to offers for the first time in several years. In 2011, the market stabilized. Still, prices (for both sales and rentals) remain down from their peaks. Owners, though, haven't been willing to admit that, at least not publicly. As a result, a lot of them have had their houses for sale for very extended periods.

All that aside, I'm more short-term bullish on the future of Panama's property market than that of any other country. Wherever you buy, you want to buy on the dips if you can, and that's the situation in Panama. Where, specifically, in this country should you consider? That depends on why you're shopping.

Panama's Best Investment Buys

If you're an investor-buyer with a long-term view, I'd recommend focusing your search on the western-facing coast of this country's Azuero Peninsula. Panama's western Azuero coast boasts some of the country's most beautiful beaches but remains largely undiscovered and underdeveloped. Barely populated, this long stretch of Pacific shoreline is dotted with one small town after another, with not one of note. The road is paved all the way to the bottom of the peninsula; otherwise, there's little infrastructure of note either. Local restaurants seat six or eight diners at a time and serve one or two menu items a day, typically for $2 or $3 a plate. Local *cantinas* serve local beer (for $1) and *seco* (the local firewater). There's no shopping, Dominos doesn't deliver, and your cell phone probably won't work. In the rainy season, the roads, including the paved coastal highway, can become impassable. Hard to get around, nowhere to go, and nothing to spend your money on when you get there. This is an edge-of-nowhere outpost and also Panama's most affordable life-at-the-beach option. You could rent a small house here for $150 or $200 per month and live on a total monthly budget of $600 or $700.

I predict that all of that is going to change. Over the coming five to seven years, I believe that values along this coast will appreciate notably, because this coastline sits at the current edge of the country's path of progress. Many who come to Panama do so for the beach. The most expensive beach choices are those nearest Panama City. The farther you travel from Panama City, the less developed the coast. About three hours outside Panama City, you reach the eastern-facing coast of the Azuero Peninsula, already being developed. Development typically equals appreciation. Azuero's west coast has yet to see much of either, but it's the logical next step.

Panama's Best Retiree Buys

For a small country, Panama offers a great diversity of lifestyle options, from cosmopolitan in Panama City (the only legitimate city in Central America) to both Pacific and Caribbean coastal (both developed and seriously not) and highland choices (again, both full amenity and "local"). If you're a retiree-buyer, I'd be surprised if you couldn't find the lifestyle you're looking for somewhere in Panama. The most developed retiree destination in Panama is Boquete, named by the AARP as the world's top retirement haven in 1995. As I've mentioned, Boquete is a place where you could export the American Dream retirement lifestyle with you, thanks to the welcoming population of foreign retirees and the developed infrastructure and amenities. And, as everywhere in Panama, prices in Boquete are down from their pre-2008 peaks.

Growth Buy 2: Colombia—Don't Tell Anyone, but Pablo Escobar Is Dead

"'¡Bájense!' shouted the man in the green fatigues, as he told us to get off the bus. Then, just in case the two Americans on board were slow to understand, he waved his machine gun at the door while looking our way. 'Hombres aquí . . . mujeres allá,' he said, as he and his group separated the male and female passengers for frisking purposes (even though all the available friskers were guys). I looked in front of the bus and saw that they'd dragged a large, freshly cut tree across the road to stop traffic. I also noticed tiny Colombian flags sewn on to the backs of their camouflage shirts, just below the collars, telling me, with relief, that they belonged to the Colombian army . . . the 'good guys.'

"After a brief frisking and an inspection of the bus (to make sure there were no bombs on board), they let us proceed on our way to our destination, the colonial city of Popayán."

That's how a friend relays his first experience in Colombia, in mid-2006. By this time, the country had begun to turn the corner, thanks, mostly, to Alvaro Uribe, the president at the time, who, since taking office in 2002, had made it his mission to fight organized terrorism. Still, travel in Colombia in the mid-2000s was an adventure.

Today there's far less reason to be concerned about safety. Unsafe areas, although they do still exist, are the exception, not the rule, including in Medellín, the city that, for decades, was the world's most notorious drug-cartel capital. Pablo Escobar, the billionaire godfather of the Medellín drug trade, and his goons reigned over this city, terrifying its citizens. But that's all history. Colombians today, including those in Medellín, are focused on a bright future and are less and less distracted by the darker aspects of their past. No, the drug and gang culture hasn't disappeared altogether, but Pablo Escobar is dead, shot and killed in 1993. Colombia has made dealing with its drug-related problems a priority since and seems to be having greater success curtailing the associated violence than other countries (including Mexico, for example). In 2010, the *New York Times* "Travel" section included Colombia on its list of "The 31 Places to Go," opening the door for the mainstream traveler to start noticing what Colombia has to offer, from the one-of-a-kind walled city of Cartagena to the colonial charm of Popayán, from the hip clubs of Bogotá to the upscale cafés of Medellín.

In May 2011, Sam Zell, perhaps the world's foremost real estate investor, made a prediction. Zell said: "If I were to identify today the next focus point for real estate investment, it would be Colombia." In September 2011, Zell made his first $75 million investment in this country. Then Carlos Slim, the world's richest man according to *Forbes* magazine, said he's seeking to boost his investments in Colombia because of the country's open policy on oil exploration, its mineral assets, and its growing middle class. Zell and Slim have marked the return of the professional investor to this country. Validating their positions, Standard and Poor's restored Colombia's investment grade rating in 2011. Moody's followed suit a few months later.

For the big money and the professional investor, all the news from Colombia is good. For the smaller, private investor or retiree, change happens more slowly when it comes to well-entrenched stereotypes like the one that shadows this country. The Medellín Cartel, long dismantled, lives on in books, movies, and our collective imagination. Pablo Escobar was shot and killed by Colombian security forces (not Harrison Ford), but it seems most folks haven't gotten the word. The lingering misperceptions are good news for global property investors. If the world were aware of what's really on offer in Colombia, from the lifestyle, safety, and security to the solid economy, energy exports, and strong currency, real estate prices would be a lot higher than they are, and individual investors like you and me wouldn't have the opportunities that we have. Once the images of Pablo Escobar (and Harrison Ford) fade, today's seriously undervalued real estate valuations will go with them.

The reality on the ground in Medellín today is smartly dressed business-people coming and going from their offices, women shopping and running errands, children riding bicycles and Rollerblading in the parks, and couples wandering from restaurant to bar to nightclub. The reality is that Medellín is a peaceful, tranquil, welcoming place. If you Google it, you'll find that the city's murder rate continues to be high on a global scale, but the important insight to recognize is that the violence and killing is gang on gang. Those in the drug trade are mostly killing each other. Innocent bystanders do get hurt or killed as well, sometimes, but the trouble areas are contained. Nobody can guarantee that the drug gangs will never again have the power and the reach that they once had in this city back in the days of Pablo Escobar. However, I can tell you that the people of Medellín have no interest in losing control of their home again. *Paisas,* as they are called, take enormous pride in their beautiful city.

Most of the world has no idea of all this. Thanks to their long-standing reputations as danger spots, Colombia in general and Medellín in particular have remained off the world's radar as retirement or investment destinations, leaving the local real estate market to the locals. The result is that property prices are a tremendous value on a global scale. You can find livable older properties in excellent neighborhoods for less than $1,000 a square meter; in more local neighborhoods, prices can be half that. Top-of-the-line new construction in the heart of the city (there is a lot of it, thanks to the strong economy and expanding middle class) is selling for as much as $2,000 a square meter, but, even at that high-end valuation, it's a great buy, given the quality of both the construction and the city where it's located. Comparable apartments in comparable neighborhoods in more recognized markets would sell for twice these figures or more.

As the stigma of the drug wars diminishes and more people visit Medellín to see the city for themselves, as more international businesses relocate to Medellín, and as retirees discover all this city has to offer, real estate prices will pop, making this one of very few markets worldwide where I believe capital appreciation is a reasonable short-term expectation. Values are up 15 percent, on average, in the past two years and should continue steadily up at this rate.

Important forces at work in this market are the foreign mining and oil industries, which have helped Colombia's economy to continue to expand even while much of the world struggles through recession and worse. Executives working for these foreign outfits operating in Colombia need furnished rentals for anywhere from a month to a year. They want high-quality properties in convenient, central locations, and they are on expense accounts, meaning they can afford to pay for what they want.

The entire country is a growth market full of opportunity. Most interesting, though, for the small individual property buyer, I believe, is Medellín. It is worth your attention if your agenda is investment, retirement, lifestyle, or, as it should be, a combination of all three, because it is both a growth market and a really nice place to be. The European undertones in Medellín are strong, from the way the women dress to the way people greet you in passing on the street. This is South America, not Central America, and the differences between the two regions can be striking. Medellín is a green city, with trees, plants, and small gardens everywhere. It's architecturally consistent and pleasing. Most every building is constructed of red brick and topped with red clay roof tiles. The overall effect is delightful, especially when viewed from some elevation (the surrounding mountainsides, for example).

Medellín is also remarkably clean. In the central neighborhoods, you see no litter anywhere. The metro, a point of pride for the population of Medellín and a great way to get around parts of the city, is spotless and like new. There's no shortage of things to do in this town, both outdoorsy and more cerebral. This is an industrial, economic, and financial center for the country, but also a literary and an artistic one. Newspapers, radio networks, publishing houses, an annual poetry festival, an international jazz festival, an international tango festival, an annual book fair, and, back in 1971, Colombia's answer to Woodstock, the Festival de Ancon, all have chosen Medellín as their base. The main attraction at the Museo de Antioquia is the Botero Collection, which is bolstered by the further collection of 23 monumental sculptures by this artist (a son of Medellín) exhibited in the Plaza Botero, in front of the museum. Finally, the climate in Medellín is about as good as it gets, with moderate temperatures and very low humidity year-round.

Medellín Market Downsides

On the other hand, investors in Medellín have a currency risk. Colombia's peso moves daily up and down against the U.S. dollar. This is not necessarily a negative; depending when you buy, it could work to your advantage. Regardless, it's something to understand before taking a position. Investors also should understand that Colombia imposes exchange controls, meaning you have to be careful how you bring money into the country. Report it incorrectly, incompletely, or not at all, and you could have trouble when you try to take it (both your capital invested and any associated profits) back out of the country down the road. This fact shouldn't keep you from buying in Colombia, but the currency controls are one important issue to discuss in detail with your attorney before transferring funds into the country.

Colombia is not a tax haven. Income and capital gains are both taxed at a rate of up to 33 percent, and the country imposes a wealth tax (which shouldn't affect the typical investor). You could pay tax of as much as 60 percent if you purchase a car here, and sales tax is 16 percent. Another lifestyle downside is the language. You won't get far in Medellín if you *hablas nada de español* (speak no Spanish).

As anywhere, it comes down to your priorities. Maybe, given your personal circumstances, the tax situation living in Colombia wouldn't be an issue for you. Maybe you embrace the challenge of communicating day to day in a second language. Maybe, for you, the near-perfect weather, the beauty of the setting and of the city itself, the friendliness of the people, and the affordable cost of living are enough to warrant a closer look at the idea of spending time long term in Medellín. Or maybe you're intrigued by the opportunity to rent a comfortable apartment in this appealing city for $300 per month or less or to invest in an apartment of your own for $60,000 or $70,000. Those are absolutely low figures on a global scale.

If you're a straight-up investor-buyer, the potential for capital appreciation bundled with the very realistic expectation of double-digit net annual returns from a rental investment property could easily make up for the potential hassles associated with bringing money into this country. Rental returns are high thanks in part to a faster rate of growth in the tourism market than in apartment prices. As demand and occupancies have expanded and values have held steady, some properties have been generating net cash flow of as much as 15 percent per year, making this one of the most appealing rental investment markets in the world.

Remember, though, that yields this high generally are unsustainable. When rental returns reach levels like these, one of two things typically happens. Rental income diminishes, as a result of a drop either in rental prices or in occupancy rates, or property prices rise. In this case, I predict that property prices will rise. Rental prices are already low, and, while more investors are being attracted to the market (creating more inventory), demand will continue to outpace supply for some time for two reasons. First, the steady increase in tourism in Medellín will help to absorb additional inventory as it becomes available. Second, it's illegal to rent an apartment short term in Medellín unless the majority of owners of a given building agree to allow it. Rental managers and others are lobbying to have this law repealed. Meantime, owners are prohibited from renting apartments for less than one month at a time, helping to suppress supply.

Colombia's Best Investment Buys

The investor-buyer in Medellín should focus on resales. Your up-front costs are lower, and the fact that the unit is older shouldn't affect your occupancy rates.

The best location in the city from an investment apartment point of view is the broader El Poblado area, centered around Parque Lleras but also including the Zona Rosa, the Milla de Oro (the Golden Mile, with lots of shopping, malls, and restaurants), and the areas east (up the mountainside). You can buy for less in other neighborhoods, but this extended area is the safest bet for the investor-buyer.

Colombia's Best Retiree Buys

The center of Medellín around Parque Lleras and the Golden Mile are also a good place to focus your search if you're buying for part-time or retirement use. Living in this part of the city, you'd be able to take full advantage of all that Medellín has to offer, often even within walking distance. However, if you're a retiree-buyer, I'd suggest another option, too, a small colonial town called El Retiro, about an hour up the mountain from Medellín, in the direction of the international airport. El Retiro, home to about 6,000 people and four beautiful Spanish colonial churches, including the oldest in the region, is a place that has managed to remain a world apart. El Retiro could be compared favorably with Granada or León, Nicaragua, minus the midday heat, or Cuenca, Ecuador, although more accessible and, thanks to its size, cozier. El Retiro is also a bargain, even compared with those other bargain-priced colonial cities. You could own one of this town's old colonial-style houses for $40,000 or $50,000. An awful lot of charm for not a lot of money.

Growth Buy 3: Mongolia—Boomtown at the End of the Earth

Buy real estate in Mongolia? That must be the punch line to some joke, right?

Nope. Mongolia has been a distant blip on my radar for at least five years, primarily because of the country's expanding mining industry. Growing numbers of foreign executives are going to need housing, I figure, as Mongolia continues to enjoy a mining boom that is expected to last decades at least, making this one of the very few markets in the world today that is expanding quickly and that should continue to expand for both the short and the longer term. On the other hand, this country boasts one of the world's harshest climates. It's a place worth seeing once, but if there are lifestyle benefits here, I haven't found them. I don't see a big Retire to Mongolia market emerging, but that's beside the point here. Buy Mongolia is an investment tip, not a lifestyle recommendation, and it's an investment tip that any investor-buyer with an appetite for risk should consider.

Mongolia is a fledgling democracy, in existence only since 1990. Prior to that, this country was a client state of the U.S.S.R. During the almost 70 years of Soviet influence, Mongolia did enjoy some benefits, including the construction of a transnational railway, advances in literacy and education, and an improved infrastructure. On the other hand, many intellectuals and other perceived enemies of the Soviet Union were killed or sent off to gulags, people were forbidden to practice their religion, agricultural and economic pursuits were placed under central government control, and freedom of the press was abolished. When *perestroika* took hold, Mongolia was one of the first countries to recognize the opportunity it presented and to strike out on its own.

Since that time, Mongolia's new government has tried to embrace democracy and a free-market economy, but it has been a difficult transition. Historically, Mongolia has been a land of nomads; however, over the past two decades, a huge migration surge has taken place, to Ulaanbaatar, which has developed into the only large city in this remote, landlocked country.

Foreigners have migrated to this spot, as well, and the city's population has exploded, doubling in the past three years alone. What's the draw? Huge untapped reserves of natural resources, including significant deposits of copper, coal, gold, iron ore, and uranium. Over the past 10 years, large mining companies from China, Australia, Canada, and Korea have been moving in to lay the groundwork for the extraction of these minerals, and Mongolians have been migrating here with the hope of finding work in construction, mining, or some related support service industry.

The first challenge has been to improve the country's infrastructure. The few roads that existed were little more than dirt tracks; housing and services were inadequate to accommodate the influx of foreign workers and investors. Today, the relatively small city center is awash with new construction—business centers, banks, and luxury high-rise condominiums—while the outlying areas are given over to large *ger* encampments, the round felt yurt-like tents used by the nomads who have moved here from the countryside in search of wealth.

All the foreign investment (foreign direct investment has surged in the past few years, growing from $25 million in 1997 to $1.02 billion in 2010) has translated into Mongolia's status as one of the fastest-growing economies in the world. In 2010, the GDP growth rate was 6.4 percent. GDP surged by 17.3 percent in 2011, and estimated GDP growth for 2012 is 17.2 percent. With the giant Oyu Tolgoi mine beginning production in 2013, allowing access to the largest untapped copper and gold reserve on the planet, it is unlikely that these extreme growth levels will slow. In addition, Mongolia also has huge untapped reserves of coal. With China purchasing up to 22 million tons of coal per month, it's safe to say that Mongolia has a long-term customer to the south. Bottom line, Mongolia should see double-digit GDP growth rates for years to come.

Although Mongolia is one of the poorest countries in Asia, and many recent immigrants coming from the steppes, deserts, and mountains to Ulaanbaatar are living at the most extreme levels of poverty, there is an emerging middle class and an expanding segment of the population that qualifies as wealthy. Today, walking through downtown Ulaanbaatar, you see shiny new Humvees and Range Rovers, Mongolian men in smart suits, and women wearing designer dresses and high heels. Everyone is busy, moving through the city with a purpose, off to their jobs at investment banks and other businesses catering to the new economy.

At the heart of the boom is the ballooning mining industry, which is creating other opportunities for foreign investors, specifically real estate investment opportunities. With the continuing influx of well-paid foreign executives and the growing number of wealthy and middle-class Mongolians, residential and commercial real estate prices have been surging. New developments are springing up throughout the city, and rental returns are as high as 15 or 16 percent per year from cash flow alone. On top of this, property values in Ulaanbaatar have been appreciating at a rate of 25 percent per year and more for the past few years, and this growth is expected to continue.

Land ownership is severely restricted in Mongolia (this is one exception to the no-government-regulation reality here). Mongolians can own no more than one-eighth of a hectare, and foreigners are not allowed to own land at all. Remember, this is a country of nomads. Herd animals need to be able to roam freely in search of good grazing, and their owners must be able to follow them. Private land borders would get in the way of this. When Mongolians do settle in one place, that land is typically leased by the local government to the user. It is possible for foreigners to lease land; a land lease in this case would typically be valid for 15 to 60 years and could be extended by up to 40 additional years.

I wouldn't recommend leasing land. However, it is possible for foreigners to own condominiums in this country, and this is the current opportunity for the investor-buyer with an appetite for quick profits and tolerance for big risk. When you purchase a condo/apartment in Ulaanbaatar, you'll be issued title to that property in the form of what is called an immovable property certificate. With this, you have the right to sell the property, to use it for collateral, or to rent it. The real estate market at this time is mainly for apartments and condos; however, some new freestanding homes are being constructed, and it's only a matter of time before upscale gated communities form new neighborhoods. These could be purchased as well, without restriction, by foreigners.

Current Values

Condominiums designed with expatriates in mind are selling, at the low end, for $2,100 per square meter, meaning a capital requirement of $130,000 to $150,000 minimum. Buy preconstruction, and you can stage your payments over a year or longer. At the other end of the spectrum, top-end luxury condos command high prices, and the most exclusive penthouses are currently being offered for about $7,000 per square meter (meaning capital requirements in the millions). The average per-square-meter price for high-end residential property is currently about $4,000.

Ulaanbaatar has the distinction of being the coldest capital city in the world. People don't move here for the weather, and neither do they live here year-round if they can avoid it. As a result, developers assume their market is not the individual end user who intends to remain in a unit indefinitely but the corporations (mostly mining) that are rotating staff through this part of the world as needed. For this reason, units are usually sold fully furnished, with all fixtures and fittings in place. This makes for turnkey investing and means you don't have to invest a lot of time or additional capital to get a place ready to rent.

As anywhere, not all locations are equal if you're buying for rental return. The best choices in this context are in areas that appeal to expat executives and wealthy locals—neighborhoods near the embassies, the National Amusement Park, and other parts of the city that are far from the *ger* encampments. Many of the condo complexes that are being developed in these locations have embraced the expatriate concept. Everything an expat family needs can be found on-site, including restaurants, bars, grocery stores, dry cleaners, and fitness clubs. This is a real plus when it's snowing, the Siberian winds are howling, and it's minus 30 degrees Fahrenheit outside.

Much of the city is a construction site; meanwhile, there is a shortage of high-end housing, and luxury units are now renting for $17 to $23 per square meter per month. This translates to a return from rental income of between 10 and 16 percent per annum. Commercial property is netting similar returns. Current cash flow from top-end retail is 13 percent per year and better. As an example, a 200-square-meter retail unit is on the market now for $3,025 per square meter, or a total cost of about $600,000. The projected annual income from this property is estimated at about $80,000. Annual capital appreciation for this kind of property has been running at about 30 percent. Combined, these rental yields and capital appreciation rates translate to an almost unbelievable return.

That level of return on investment (ROI) won't continue indefinitely and doesn't come without risk. This is very much a developing market, and the associated challenges can be major. For example, the city provides central hot water to housing units for heating and bathing. However, water lines are repaired during the summer, and the hot water can be shut off until the maintenance is completed. Friends visiting Ulaanbaatar recently told me that they happened to stay in one of the neighborhoods where water mains were being repaired. They didn't see a drop of hot water emerge from the tap during their entire two weeks in the city. "And, even in the summer," my friend pointed out, "taking a cold-water shower in Ulaanbaatar is like washing with ice water!" Luxury residences now being built in the city have their own hot water systems and electric generators, and this is something you should ask about for any building where you consider investing.

By any definition, Mongolia is a remote country. It has the distinction of being the least densely populated country in the world and shares borders with only two countries—Russia and China. Coming to Mongolia by land can only reasonably be accomplished by rail, as the roads in Mongolia are few and far between. The Genghis Khan International Airport, located just outside Ulaanbaatar, is currently, and for the foreseeable future, the only major international airport in the country. There are no direct commercial flights from the Western Hemisphere to Mongolia. Traveling from the West, you must first fly to China, Korea, Russia, or Japan and take a connecting flight to Ulaanbaatar from there.

Like any early-stage developing market, Mongolia imposes very few restrictions on anything. This is a plus and a minus. On one hand, it means little government red tape to navigate when purchasing property. For example, you are not required to have a notary present when signing a contract, and neither are you required to have an attorney present during any stage of a property transaction. On the other hand, the almost utter lack of regulation means you are on your own to protect yourself and your investment. So, although you don't need an attorney, I'd recommend you invest in one. (The cost should be less than $1,000 per transaction.) No registration is required for someone to call himself a real estate agent in this country, which means you have no assurance that the guy helping you with your purchase has any idea what he's doing or can be counted on to protect your interests. Do your homework. Look for an agency with a good reputation, strong references, and a proven track record. Ask your attorney for a recommendation.

Much like a boomtown in the old American West, Ulaanbaatar is definitely rough around the edges. Although there are signs of gentrification, the crime rate is above average and air pollution is often well above levels considered healthy. The infrastructure, though improving, remains primitive in many ways. Health care is substandard. An expensive SOS International Medical Clinic services the needs of expatriates, but, in case of serious illness or injury, the recommendation is to go abroad for treatment.

Meanwhile, any way you want to measure it, this town is booming. The opportunities on offer are great, and the window for getting in before valuations become silly is closing. As one expat businessman puts it, "We've spent 10 years getting ready to take these minerals out of the ground, and now we're almost ready to start. In one year, we're going to have lots of copper, iron ore, coal, gold, and uranium. You're going to see a lot of Rolls-Royces on the streets soon, as minerals are sold, and the stock market rises. In a few more years, this place will look like Qatar."

Growth Buy 4: Brazil—Big Upside Potential but Unique Challenges

Brazil belongs on any list of growth markets. It presents opportunity for both the investor and anyone looking for a second home in the sun. However, buying in Brazil can be tricky, making it an interesting country to study. As in Colombia, the buyer in Brazil has to navigate constant fluctuations of the currency exchange rate, in this case between the real and the U.S. dollar. Also as in Colombia, Brazil imposes exchange controls, meaning you must be very careful about how you bring money into the country or you could have trouble when the time comes to take it (and any associated profits) out. I know investors who tell horror stories about their experiences trying to repatriate funds from Brazil, including one American who tried to enlist the U.S. embassy as an ally in his battle. FYI: The U.S. embassy can't really help with this kind of thing. This is what your local attorney is for. Satisfy yourself that your attorney understands the complexities associated with moving money in and out of this country. If he or she doesn't, find another.

Unlike in Colombia, however, and very important to understand when shopping for real estate in Brazil, it's not uncommon in this country to find developers offering financing with a very low down payment. This presents a great and unique opportunity for leverage; it also creates its own set of risks.

A few years ago, I knew of a well-publicized launch of a preconstruction project in Fortaleza, on Brazil's northern coast. Promoters had secured a block of condos with exclusive rights to market them prior to the public launch. The developer agreed to extend a 20 percent discount to these early buyers and to provide developer financing with only 1 percent down. The condos were intended to serve the business traveler and tourist market as short-term rentals, with an eye to the anticipated demand created by the 2014 World Cup taking place in Fortaleza. The offer was well received, and scores of investors participated.

When the official public launch was held for invited local real estate agents, the units were offered at a 5 percent discount, meaning the early buyers had bought for 15 percent less than the initial public price. As a result, some investors made good money. Some, though, saw only modest gains, some lost money, all things considered, and many are still holding their units. What's the difference in the outcome to date?

The terms of purchase. The cash buyers fared best. The U.S. dollar was relatively strong at the time of purchase (1.95 reais per U.S. dollar), and then dropped over the following year, to 1.79 reais per U.S. dollar. Cash buyers who sold their units made 9 percent on the exchange rate alone, plus approximately 15 percent on the value of the property. For a buyer selling after one year, those two things compounded to mean a gross gain of more than 25 percent, before deducting transaction costs.

The complicating factor was the developer financing, for a couple of reasons. First, as buyers taking advantage of the developer financing were paying over time, they were exposed to the dollar's decline during the finance period. They had bought in with a fixed monthly payment of 1,450 reais. Over the course of the following year, this payment increased from $743 to $810 per month in dollar terms.

In addition, making time payments anywhere in Brazil exposes you to something called the INCC, a government-established inflation adjustment that allows builders to keep up with ongoing increases in the cost in materials and labor during any construction period. In the particular year following purchase in this case, the INCC added a total of 5.91 percent.

Do the math and you understand the problem. The time-payment buyer was left with a total gain (in dollar terms) of just 9.3 percent, compared with more than 25 percent for the cash buyer, before subtracting transaction costs, travel expenses for visits to the property, and so on. Net gains after one year in these cases were modest, in some cases nonexistent.

I think this is an important case study because it seems to fly in the face of traditional wisdom regarding how to make money investing in real estate. You make more money with leverage, right? When buying overseas, as this example shows, this is not always the case, though it's important to note that things could have turned out differently in our example. Had the dollar strengthened during the period in question, cash buyers would have suffered, while time-payment buyers would have watched as their payment went down and unpaid balance shrunk, in dollar terms.

That's buying preconstruction on time from a developer in Brazil. A friend, Chris, took a different route entirely when he bought in this country. He shopped on the local market and did quite well with the purchase of a house on the beach. One reason, I'd say, is because he didn't approach the purchase purely as a profit opportunity. Chris found a comfortable house right on a beach he loved for what he determined to be a greatly undervalued price. He and his wife, Janet, made the purchase believing that they would realize a good financial return if and when they decided to sell; however, more than that, they bought because they'd found a place where they wanted to be.

Chris and Janet invested in a 2,000-square-foot house only 25 feet from the high-tide line on a reef-protected beach for just under $62,000 (at the exchange rate at the time). The home was located on the causeway-connected island of Itamaracá, in Northeast Brazil's state of Pernambuco. Island rental histories indicated that the property could earn in excess of 6 percent net annual return as a vacation rental on the local Brazilian market. Chris bought with a realistic expectation of capital gains and a realistic backup expectation of cash flow.

It wasn't long after Chris and Janet moved in, however, before word got out. Other foreigners from the United States, Canada, and the United Kingdom started buying up the remaining beachfront properties on the island. As inventory dwindled, prices went up. At the same time, the dollar began to fall against the Brazilian real, making Chris' property more valuable in dollar terms. After just 10 months, Chris sold his house for 78 percent more than he'd paid. That's a gross annualized gain of 93.7 percent.

Expenses associated with the purchase, the sale, and capital improvements Chris made totaled about $19,000. Taking that into account, the net gain was almost 47 percent, and the net annualized return was better than 56 percent. Here are the actual numbers:

Sales and Price Data	Exchange/USD	Price (*reais*)	Price (USD)
Purchase (3/5/09)	R$ 2.3918	R$ 148,000	$61,878
Sale (1/6/10)	R$ 1.7240	R$ 190,000	$110,209
		R$ 42,000	$48,331
Actual gain (gross)	38.7 percent	28.4 percent	78.1 percent
Annualized gain (gross)		34.1 percent	93.7 percent
Total cost of purchase			$7,174
Total costs of sale (negotiated settlement)			$10,000
Legal fees			$650
Advertising			$150
Modifications to property			$1,389
Total costs			$19,363
Net gain in dollars			$28,968
Actual net gain			46.8 percent
Annualized net gain			56.2 percent

A very successful investment experience by anyone's standards. Part of the success here, as in our preconstruction developer purchase example, is owed to the fact that Chris bought for cash. The fall of the dollar following his purchase worked in his favor. The reais he walked away with after selling bought more dollars back home. Had he financed the purchase, his U.S. dollar payments would have gone up as the dollar weakened.

Chris was also successful because he was on the ground. Prior to buying, he spent time scouting the nooks and crannies of the Brazilian coast. This was how he found the island of Itamaracá. Discovering good local deals is much easier if you've got time for firsthand exploring. And firsthand exploring can be a big part of the fun.

Chris' discovery of Itamaracá was a big deal. Finding an undervalued market with a dwindling inventory takes time and experience, and Chris enjoyed big rewards for his effort in the form of capital appreciation. Chris was also lucky. His capital returns were compounded by a currency gain. This no one can project or predict, and, as with the buyers in Fortaleza, this could have gone the other way. A strengthening dollar could have eroded Chris' gains, leaving him with more modest profits.

When I asked him about his experience buying and selling in Brazil, though, Chris's initial response didn't have anything to do with the profits he'd earned or the currency gain he'd enjoyed. "It was one of the best years my wife and I have spent," he told me, "living in that house on that beautiful beach. We'll always remember that time."

That's a successful real estate investment overseas.

8 Buy Agri-Profits

Eighteenth- and nineteenth-century apartments in central Paris . . . and land."

Those were the recommendations from a friend, a Frenchman whose opinion I respect, when I asked for his investment advice.

"Centuries-old bijou real estate in a brand-name city like Paris and productive agricultural land on which to grow corn, soybeans, wheat, alfalfa, fruit trees, grape vines, or timber," Frank replied without hesitation. "Because the world is always going to need those things. The demand is only going to increase, no matter what."

Productive land is the ultimate hard asset. Unlike a lot in a development community or a plot in the middle of a commercial district, productive land always retains the potential for yield. By definition, productive land is land where you could produce something of marketable value. When whatever you plant or herd reaches maturity, you harvest and sell. Productive land also provides diversification and can be part of a legacy wealth plan.

This can be about farming, but I'm not suggesting you pick up a hoe. You have good options for taking advantage of this classic diversification strategy without ever getting your hands dirty. Specifically, I recommend three productive land investments that you can participate in without having to learn much of anything about how to grow and harvest crops: timber (specifically teak), coconuts, and farmland.

Agri-Buy 1: Panama—Where Money Grows on (Teak) Trees

Historically, timber has enjoyed the best risk/reward ratio of any investment sector. Depending on whose chart of historical returns you consult, timber as an asset category has produced an annualized ROI in the range of 12 to 15 percent per year every year since they started keeping records of investment risk versus return. A friend calls timber "a long-held secret of the world's wealthiest people." It's a low-volatility hedge against inflation and an asset class that operates independent of the stock market.

On top of this, timber is a commodity that will always have a market and that doesn't have to be harvested at a particular time. That means that, if prices for your wood are less than you want or expected them to be, you can leave your trees in the ground so they can continue to grow until prices reach a level you like better.

Here's how a direct timber investment should work: You buy the land. A management company plants trees on it and maintains them for you. They take care of everything—from insect and weed control to thinnings—until harvest time. Come harvest time, the management company organizes the cutting and the sale of the trees. The revenues from the harvest go to you, as the owner. After the trees have been harvested, you still own the land, meaning you can replant and start the process over for another harvest.

I'm oversimplifying, but the point is that you want to be buying the land, not only the trees. Your returns can be good, even better, investing in trees alone, but, in the end, you are subsidizing the land ownership for the tree farmer. Once your trees are harvested, you're done, left without any residual asset, and productive land is all about the long-term hard asset. You also don't want to be buying shares of the operating company that owns and manages the land and the timber. Buying shares, again, you're undermining the opportunity you're meant to be capitalizing on, buying not a real productive asset but into a company. You have no control over the land, the timber, or how the business is operated. The only thing you control is the timing for when you sell your shares, and, once they've been sold, you're left with nothing. A productive land investment should always leave you with something.

For my money, teak is about the surest timber investment you can make. It is indigenous to only four countries—Burma, Thailand, Laos, and India. For centuries, the kings of Burma and Thailand considered teak a royal tree. Today, Burma, home to the last remaining natural teak forests, all of which are the property of the government, is the largest global exporter of premium teak, producing about 80 percent of world supply. These remaining natural forests are being logged at a rapid rate. Some predictions are that Burmese forests could be logged completely in the next few years, meaning the growing world demand (for outdoor furniture, flooring, boats, etc.) would have to be fulfilled by teak plantation production. And, right now, there aren't a lot of teak plantations worldwide.

Although trees take years rather than months to grow to a harvestable size, they also can carry less risk of being completely wiped out than, say, a tomato crop. Teak trees have been farmed in plantations for hundreds of years starting with plantations in Southeast Asia. Today, teak plantations can be found in a band around the earth between 20 degrees north and 20 degrees south of the Equator. This includes Southeast Asia, India, Central America, Brazil, and parts of Africa. In addition to the required climate, you also need good soil to get decent growth rates for teak and a definitive dry season of at least four months. The dry season is when the hardwood in the center of the trees is made. Taking a look at a world map and all things considered (the ideal growing requirements, the ease of investment, the cost of investment, the opportunities for investment, and the tax implications), Panama jumps out as a top choice for investing in teak. This country is one of a handful of places in the world where you can grow premium teak trees. In addition, Panama is very pro-investor, home to a number of managed plantations, and, because it is interested in promoting forestry, makes the proceeds from related investments tax free.

Owning a couple of hectares of teak trees could be a very profitable concept. At the same time, owning a couple of random hectares of any kind of tree doesn't make much investment sense. For this kind of investment to work, you need trees that are managed professionally by an outfit with experience in both growing and harvesting the crop in question and access to a ready market for the end product. Few of us are prepared to invest the time that would be required to understand the industry and actually run the farm. I've known investors who have simply planted some teak trees and left them to grow. The results have never been good.

Fire is one key risk of a timber investment. Teak trees, however, are effectively immune from forest fires after about three years of growth. Years ago, I toured a timber plantation. The manager walked me through a section of the plantation where, a few years earlier, a wildfire had swept through. In that area at the time of the fire were four- and five-year-old plantings of cedar, mahogany, and teak. Nearly all the cedar and mahogany trees were lost to the fire, but not one teak tree. I saw the teak growing still.

Insects are another risk. As with fire, though, teak is fairly immune after three years.

Perhaps the biggest drawback to investing in trees, teak or otherwise, is the investment term. Unlike cattle, for example, which mature in less than a year and then can be taken to market, you have to wait 10 to 25 years before you see any real return from a timber investment. Eucalyptus matures in maybe 13 years, pine in 15 to 20. It can take as long as 25 years before teak is ready for harvest, meaning it is definitely a legacy investment, made as much for your kids and grandkids as for yourself. Thinnings are done several times during the growth cycle, but they bring limited revenue. The full harvest is done sometime between year 17 and year 25, depending on growth rates, which depend on soil and weather.

Although you generally have to wait at least 17 years to harvest teak trees, that doesn't mean you have to wait that long to cash out of your investment. Investors with shorter time horizons look to purchase established plantations. If you find yourself needing or wanting to cash out of your teak plantation before the full harvest, buyers are out there. This is a more liquid market than you might imagine. The reverse is also true. If you are looking for a shorter investment period, you could buy an older plantation. This strategy shortens the investment horizon but requires a larger initial investment. Your annualized returns can be about the same.

As I mentioned, several managed teak plantations operate in Panama. The important thing to understand when considering an investment in any one of them is whether you, as an investor, take title to the land where your trees are growing. For most of the plantations in this country, this is not the case. One where you do take title to the land is United Nature, operating since 1993 and with about 3,000 hectares of teak under management. As an investor with United Nature, you could decide when to take the final harvest (although I'd say the sensible thing would be to take the management team's advice on this), and you could sell your piece of the plantation whenever you wanted.

Agri-Buy 2: Brazil—Cuckoo for Coconuts

Coconuts are a multipurpose crop. You can get a multitude of products out of one of these nuts, from water to meat, husk to oil. Each product has a different use and a different market. The biggest demands are for the water and the oil.

Coconuts are ubiquitous in Brazil and so is the water they produce. On any beach along this country's long coast, you can find coconut vendors hacking off the tops of coconuts, sticking a straw into each open nut, and selling the portable, natural thirst quencher to hot and sticky passersby. In the United States and Europe, coconut water is mass-produced, packaged in bottles and cans by big drink companies including Coca-Cola and Pepsi (the respective brands are Zico and O.N.E.), and sold on grocery store shelves. Their coconut water products are not marketed aggressively in the United States by either Coke or Pepsi, because neither group can get enough supply. They sell all that they are able to produce even without making any serious investment in promotions.

Coconut water alone has enough of a market to make investing in plantations of coconuts a good idea, but it's only the beginning of the investment opportunity. In addition, there's the oil, which, like the nut itself, has many potential uses, key among them being biofuel. Brazil is energy self-sufficient. It produces all the energy it needs from products within its borders, including fossil fuels, like oil and natural gas, and biofuels, from coconuts and other crops. Biofuel from coconut oil is more efficient than biofuel from corn, making it a more interesting option, and Brazil is at the forefront of efforts to use coconut oil for fuel. More than 50 percent of the cars in Brazil run on bioethanol, and 90 percent of new cars in Brazil are designed to burn biofuel. Meanwhile, coconut oil can also be used for cooking and pharmaceuticals.

A coconut also has a husk, which also can be used as a biofuel (I visited a coconut processing plant in Brazil that uses coconut husks to run the generator that powers the entire plant). Coconut husks also can be made into stuffing for mattresses and furniture. Then you have the meat, which is used for foodstuffs, including coconut milk when pressed a certain way, and the shell. You may never have seen a coconut shell, because it hides beneath the husk, but it, too, has value, as an animal feed.

With all these potential revenue streams, the investor in a coconut plantation can feel comfortable that, when his nuts are ready for harvest, he'll find a market. If folks are drinking less coconut water, maybe cosmetic companies are shopping for more oil. If biofuel prices are down, maybe pharmaceutical prices are up.

Owning a couple of hectares of coconut trees could be a very profitable concept. At the same time, as I've explained, owning a couple of random hectares of any kind of tree doesn't make much investment sense. For this kind of investment to work, you need trees that are managed professionally by an outfit that has both experience growing and harvesting the crop in question and access to a ready market for the end product. Unless you're ready to invest a lot time in understanding the industry and running the farm, owning a plantation of your own is certainly an ambitious and probably a silly idea. The more sensible option, as with teak, is to invest in a managed plantation where you own the land. This way, you have direct ownership (rather than shares of a company, which I don't recommend), while benefiting from the management company's economies of scale and expertise.

Over the years, I've looked at several tree investment opportunities. In the case of coconuts, I believe the best ones are grown in Brazil, specifically in Fortaleza, thanks to this region's soil and climate. Fortaleza has long stretches of the kind of sandy soil that coconut trees like and favorable annual rainfall levels. Plus, unlike the Philippines and India, two other big coconut-growing locales, this part of the world is removed from any treacherous storm zone, so the trees aren't exposed to damaging winds.

Despite this, there are few coconut plantations in Brazil, meaning this is a growth market with lots of room to expand. The country has the infra-structure to process coconuts for all their various uses. What are the downsides? Brazil is tightening up on restrictions related to foreign owner-ship of agricultural land. Currently, the country limits foreign ownership to 2 percent of agricultural land. This percentage is calculated state by state, which means that, in states like Rio, where foreigners have already bought a large amount of agricultural land, the 2 percent limit is close to being reached. In Ceará state, a good choice for a coconut plantation investment, few foreigners have bought agri-land, so the 2 percent cap isn't a concern. In addition, note that Brazil requires foreigners to own a minimum of 1 hectare of agri-land. The other risks of a coconut plantation investment in Brazil are to do with currency (the real moves daily versus the U.S. dollar) and exchange controls. I address both of these potential concerns in detail in Chapter 7.

I know one coconut plantation investment opportunity in Brazil that has been packaged for the small individual foreign investor. The minimum investment requirement is $60,000, which buys you 2 hectares of land in a managed plantation. The projected annualized return, net of all costs and expenses, including Brazilian income tax, is about 15 percent. This projected return is based on a price per coconut of 1.20 reais. Coconuts are sold by the kilogram. The nuts being grown on the plantation in question average 1 kilogram or more. The price being paid by the processing plant where these coconuts are being sold as of this writing is 1.34 reais per kilogram, meaning that, currently, each coconut in question is worth 1.34 reais or more, not 1.20 reais. The price changes weekly and depends on the season. Prices are higher during the Brazilian summer, because the local market demand for coconut water increases. This managed plantation investment is available from a UK-based group called Liquid Invest (http://www3 .liquid-investments.com/coco).

Agri-Buy 3: Uruguay—Cultivating Profits from the Global Race to Farmland

Warren Buffet wondered not long ago: "Would you rather own *all* the gold in the world or *all* the farmland?"

Everyone is talking about the new asset class. Farmland isn't a new asset class. It's the world's oldest asset class. However, it has become very attractive in the past several years and is going to become more attractive over the coming decade as the world's population continues to expand. We're looking at a total world population of more than 9 billion people by the middle of this century. This is translating to a global race for farmland, with some countries (such as Brazil) imposing restrictions on foreign ownership of productive land.

The old real estate investment adage recommends buying beachfront because no one will be making more of it. There's a limited supply of farmland, too, and a fast-growing demand. Farmland, therefore, is and will continue to be the world's best possible store of value. Looking at a world map, three places are most interesting in this context: Africa, Eastern Europe, and South America. Among the three regions, South America is the most competitive; Africa and Eastern Europe are more volatile, with more corruption, lack of clear rules, and restrictions on foreign ownership. In South America, Uruguay, in particular, stands out; about 95 percent of the land in this country is farmable. Until the start of this century, most of Uruguay's land was used for cattle. When farmers began to recognize the implications of the coming global population crisis, they switched from cows to soybeans (and other crops). Because Uruguayans haven't farmed their land for 200 years, it's virgin. There's been no soil degradation as in more recognized global breadbaskets.

Foreign and local investors are treated the same in Uruguay; there are no restrictions on foreign ownership or use of land, nor are there exchange controls or currency restrictions. Uruguay is a foreigner-friendly, investor-friendly place and, as a result, has enjoyed the highest rate of foreign direct investment per capita of all Latin America for the past three years.

Uruguay sees even rainfall year-round, plus the country sits on the world's largest untapped aquifer. The climate is temperate, with four mild seasons. Farmers can raise two crops per year.

Uruguay's farmland market is transparent. The entire country has been surveyed for productivity levels. Each land parcel has an ID number. You can plug this number into a map (available online: www.prenader.gub.uy /coneat) to see the productivity rating for whatever piece of land interests you. The system amounts to an MLS for farmland quality, making it uncommonly easy to compare all your options at once. The average productivity rating for the country is 100. A lower rating means you're looking at land that's really suitable for running cattle only. You want land rated 120 or 130 or better. Price correlates to productivity rating.

What could you produce? Almost anything you could imagine, from agricultural crops (soybeans, wheat, rice, etc.) to cattle or sheep, forestry (eucalyptus, pine), vineyards, olives, blueberries, and so on. None of these is a new crop to Uruguay—5 percent of the world's meat exports come from Uruguay; the country has the two biggest paper mills in the world; and Uruguay is the world's sixth-largest exporter of soybeans and fourth-largest exporter of rice. If you're buying for investment, plant soybeans (to sell to China). If you're buying for investment and for fun, try a hobby crop, like blueberries or grapes.

You could buy 50 acres to thousands of acres. One of the many unique things about farmland investing in this country is that there are brokers with access to available farm investment opportunities across the country. All things considered, farmland in Uruguay is one of the most turnkey, user-friendly property purchases you could make anywhere in the world.

What would you do with your land once you'd bought it? You could either rent it out or hire a farm manager. A farm manager is like a property manager for a rental property. He is the key to your success. In Uruguay, there are many professional farm management companies, meaning, again, your options are turnkey.

Prices for farmland in Uruguay range from $1,000 to $4,000 an acre ($2,500 to $10,000 per hectare). Again, this is tied to productivity rating. Buy as much of the most highly productive land as you can (as opposed to more of lesser rated land) with the budget you have. The better-rated land will hold its value. Your return will depend on the type of product you instruct your management company to farm. Agriculture will return 4 to 9 percent per year; cattle 3 to 6 percent per year; forestry 6 to 10 percent per year. The most productive land is to be found in the country's southwestern corner.

The option would be to lease out the land you buy. Your return this way is less but more reliable, at about 4 percent a year. Many people buy and rent out for a year, and then when they're more comfortable with the whole idea, hire a farm management company for the greater yield. Farm management companies charge 5 percent of gross sales or 10 percent of net income.

These returns don't include appreciation. Farmland in Uruguay has been appreciating at a rate of about 10 percent per year and this should continue.

Taxes related to farm revenues are low. Regular corporate income tax is a flat 25 percent in Uruguay. However, if you have a farm producing less than $240,000 per year (this would be a farm valued at $1 million or less), you pay only a capped tax of $5,125 annually. Property tax on farmland averages 0.2 percent. There's no value added tax (VAT) on most supplies and machinery nor is there VAT on the sale of farm products.

Farmland in Uruguay can be both an investment and a lifestyle, and even a retirement plan. You could buy a small working farm (say 10 to 15 acres) with a small house (say 1,500 square feet) for $300,000 to $400,000. Engage a farm management company to maximize the return from whatever crop you decide to farm while keeping perhaps some small field for your own hobby use. For more information on making a productive land investment in this country, I recommend English-speaking attorney Juan Federico Fischer with Fischer & Schickendantz, www.uruguayfarms.com. He has long experience counseling foreign investors in his country.

9

Buy Where Your Heart and Your Wanderlust Lead You—20 Countries to Consider

Perhaps you're not looking to take advantage of crisis opportunity, you're not concerned about investing for growth, and you're not in the market for a productive land play. Perhaps you're looking, simply, for a new home and a new life. Maybe you even have an idea where you'd like those things to be. Or perhaps not. Perhaps you're open to suggestions, and even confused by all the choices.

If the agenda for your adventure overseas is driven more by your heart than your calculator, here are recommendations to help focus your thinking and further your plan. Following are glimpses into 20 countries where you could relaunch your life, full- or part-time, in retirement or otherwise, for the better, while at the same time diversifying your assets with the acquisition of a place of your own that could generate cash flow from rental when you're not using it yourself. I would classify these 20 countries as the world's top live and invest overseas havens. Each is, in its way and for different reasons, a great place to be.

Argentina

In late 2001, the Argentines removed the peg between their peso and the U.S. dollar, devaluing the Argentine currency, which fell at its lowest point to 4:1 against the greenback. This crisis situation opened a window of opportunity that Lief and I took advantage of to buy in 2002 with friends, a classic-style apartment in Recoleta, one of the best addresses in the center of Buenos

Aires, for half what the place would have been valued at prior to the devaluation debacle. We rented out the apartment for six years, used it occasionally ourselves, and then sold it in 2008 to double our investment. Prices had returned to where they had been just before the previous collapse. We sold, coincidentally, near a top.

When speaking of Argentina, it's safer to refer to "a" top, rather than "the" top, as there have been many and will be many more. Bottoms, too, and we are, now, in fact, on the doorstep of another bottom. Argentina is a diverse country with lots of natural resources. It could be, should be an economic success story, and now and then, it is. It's also a case study in economic mismanagement (see Chapter 5). The ongoing problem is politics, which keep this country in a perpetual cycle of crisis and make living in Argentina anything but dull. I've read that *porteños* (the folks living in Buenos Aires) are uncommonly likely to seek regular psychotherapy, undergo cosmetic surgery, and (alas) commit suicide. Argentines are a kooky bunch. They enjoy the drama of their country, and, frankly, so do I. Buenos Aires is one of the world's brand-name cities, vibrant and full of personality, like the people who live there. Visit Buenos Aires and you will remember it always, and Buenos Aires is only the beginning of what Argentina has to offer.

Argentina makes about one-half of all the wine produced annually in South America. About half of this comes from Argentina's Mendoza region, where the landscapes of red earth and purple grapes appear eternal. Argentina's is a café culture, meaning the people value good wine, good coffee, and good conversation. The art of conversation, so alive here, could be part of the explanation for how the extremely varied Argentine population has managed to live harmoniously throughout history, despite the near constant influx and influence of immigrants, starting with the Spanish, who came in the quest for silver (*argentum* is Latin for silver). Argentina was a Spanish colony until 1816. Then came the Swiss, the Italians, and the French, who arrived with their grapes. The British arrived about this time, too, and administered the building of the country's infrastructure, including its national banking and large railway systems. In fact, trains still travel on the left-hand side of track, a last stand of British influence.

Argentina can be an ideal option for part-year living, as Argentina enjoys reverse seasons of those in the United States. The expat community is not overwhelming. You can tap into if you'd like, for friends and support, or you can make your own way among the Argentines, who are friendly, polite, and respectful. Family is a priority, yet at the same time, Argentines like to socialize. In Buenos Aires you have access to tango halls, live theater, antique fairs, art galleries, opera, ballet, symphony, and independent film festivals. Elsewhere in this enormous country is some of the best skiing and hiking in the world.

Argentina offers strong lifestyle choices, from Buenos Aires to Mendoza, but, thanks to the high inflation of the past several years, it is not cheap right now, neither the cost of living nor the cost of real estate. Wait for the next collapse (which is coming) before buying.

Belize

Warm and welcoming, independent and private. Those four perhaps seemingly contradictory adjectives best describe both Belizeans and their country. Belize is also one of the safest countries in the world, despite what you may read about it. In some neighborhoods of Belize City, gang members and drug dealers do the things that gang members and drug dealers do, but those are small, contained areas. Outside Belize City, crime is nearly nonexistent.

Belize was a colony of Britain until 1981, meaning that the people here speak English. They also value their freedom, as it's relatively new.

In the nearly 30 years that I've been spending time in this country, I've joked that "the good news from Belize is no news from Belize." This is a sleepy Caribbean nation with but 330,000 people and three highways. On the other hand, little Belize offers a whole lot of what many retirees and investors are looking for—a chance to start over on sandy, sunny shores. Prices for a bit of sand on Ambergris, the most developed of Belize's islands, are not cheap but cheaper than elsewhere in the Caribbean. Other areas to shop in this country for the beach life are Placencia, on the southern mainland coast, and Corozal, on the northern mainland coast. I favor the interior Cayo region with its Mayan ruins, caves, rivers, waterfalls, and rain forest, a frontier where self-sufficient communities are emerging and attracting like-minded folks interested in being "independent together," as a friend living in this part of the world describes it.

Belize is a small country with a small population. You'll enjoy it here if you like wide-open spaces and small-town living where everyone knows everyone. You won't like it here if you crave regular doses of culture or First World–style amenities and services. With the exception of Ambergris Caye, where the country's biggest expat community is centered, and consequently, where services to cater to foreign retirees and investors have developed, life in Belize is best described as back to basics.

Legal residency is easy to obtain in Belize, and foreign residents pay no tax in Belize on non-Belize income. I would not recommend Belize if you have a serious health concern or existing medical condition. Health care facilities and standards are improving but limited.

Brazil

Brazil is one of the hemisphere's powerhouse economies, with a strongly emerging middle class. The country is energy independent, has a solid industrial base, and is quickly becoming a world leader. Former President Lula da Silva's economic policies get much of the credit for Brazil's current enviable situation. According to the International Monetary Fund, per capita income in Brazil rose by a staggering 162.8 percent between 2001 and 2010. During da Silva's tenure, the income of the richest Brazilians rose by 10 percent, while the income of the poorest Brazilians rose a hefty 72 percent. This has had a hugely positive economic impact.

Brazil's history is one of the Americas' fascinating stories. Over the years, it was the New World's great plantation slave society, host to its first major gold rush, and ruled by the hemisphere's only empire. Brazil was settled by the Dutch, the French, and the Portuguese, and while the Portuguese ultimately gained control, all three left their cultural footprints, as did the Africans who came in slavery.

Brazil is a big country, but most of the viable lifestyle options are along the coast, from the big city of Rio de Janeiro to smaller beach towns like Florianopolis. I'd recommend taking a look at Maceió. The first Europeans to arrive here were Dutch settlers who came to Brazil to start a sugar plantation to supply the ever-increasing demand in Europe in the early 1600s. The Portuguese took control of the area in the 1650s, and the city continued to grow. Maceió soon became a major seaport, exporting timber, tobacco, coconuts, leather, and spices.

Today, Maceió is modern, clean, and elegant with miles of white sand beaches studded with colorful umbrellas and bordered by tall, swaying palms. Its warm turquoise waters gently lap the shores as beachgoers from all over enjoy the sun and sand. The town's long stretch of beachfront is the main attraction, and it's one of the best you'll find in Brazil. It's as naturally beautiful as it's possible for a beach to be, but without the bothersome vendors, beggars, and obvious sex trade that you'll find in other, better-known Brazilian beach cities. If you're in the market for cheap beachfront property, Maceió should be near the top of your list. You could buy a large, three-bedroom apartment here for less than $75,000.

Downsides to Brazil include the small English-speaking population (relative to the 200 million inhabitants), meaning that you'd have to learn Portuguese to make a success of living or investing in this country. Other downsides have to do with currency exchange rates and controls, important topics that I address in detail in Part 5.

Note that Americans need a visa to visit Brazil that must be obtained prior to arriving in the country.

Chile

With its modern four-lane highways, reliable communications, and high standard of living, Chile can be one of Latin America's easiest transitions for American expats and retirees. If not completely First World, it is not far off the mark with the second-highest gross domestic product per capita in Latin America. The country feels efficient, well run, and safe. Utilities work, buses leave on time, and you can stroll the streets without worry. According to Transparency International, Chile is also one of the least corrupt countries in the Western Hemisphere, ranking slightly behind the United States.

For American baby boomers, our introduction to Chile was the overthrow of President Salvador Allende in 1973. The aftermath of this event, the long, harsh dictatorship of General Augusto Pinochet, proved more of a shock to Chileans than to everyone else. It was largely out of character with this nation's history. Chile today is peaceful, stable, and prosperous.

Santiago, Chile's capital city, was established by Spanish conquistador Pedro de Aldivia in 1540. Over the next decade, Valdivia expanded the colony in Chile, founding La Serena in 1544. It is this town that I would suggest you consider. Santiago is a great and modern city, but the extraordinarily high levels of pollution make it an uncomfortable place to be. In La Serena, the skies are clear, with little pollution. At night the Milky Way lays a wide swath of glittering light across the skies, clearer here than practically anywhere else on Earth. For that reason, several major observatories are located in or near La Serena. The scientists who work at these facilities and their families make up a significant part of La Serena's expat community.

La Serena is a coastal community yet more temperate than tropical. Temperatures are pleasant year-round. This would not be a super-cheap option, but an affordable one and a good example of getting what you pay for. Chile in general and La Serena in particular offer a near–First World lifestyle for less overall than you'd pay in North America or Europe. The best value in La Serena is the cost of real estate. You can buy on the Pacific coast here for roughly one-quarter the cost of owning on the coast of California. One expat I know with experience in La Serena equates it to "California 40 years ago."

Colombia

Years ago, I sat around a table in a just-opened restaurant in a little-known mountain town in Panama called Boquete with a group of investors and businesspeople who were in the country, as I was, to scout opportunity. "I believe that the potential in this place for retirees is enormous," one of the gentlemen in the group (the one who had just invested in opening the restaurant where we were having dinner) theorized. "Right now, the opportunity here is for the investor and the speculator. Property prices are so undervalued. Apartments in Panama City are a screaming bargain on a global scale. Pacific beachfront, Caribbean, farmland, riverfront, this country has it all, and it's all cheap.

"Panama is still misunderstood, suffering from a lingering case of bad press," my host for the evening continued. "When you say 'Panama' to an American today, he thinks: Noriega, drug cartels, CIA intrigue. It won't be too many years before those perceptions are flipped on their head. I predict that five, seven years from now, when you say 'Panama' to the average American, he'll think: retirement. Because that's what this country is gearing up to offer—a very appealing retirement option."

That was 1999. In August 2010, the American Association of Retired Persons (AARP) named Boquete, Panama, one of the top five places in the world to retire.

In 2011, I sat around a table in a just-opened restaurant in a little-known mountain town in Colombia called Medellín with a group of investors and businesspeople who were in the country, as I was, to explore current opportunity. "Property values in this city are so undervalued," one of the gentlemen having dinner with me remarked. "I believe that apartment costs here are the lowest for any cosmopolitan city in the world on a per-square-meter basis. This is because Colombia, including Medellín, is still misunder-stood. When you say 'Medellín' to the average American, he thinks: Drugs, gangs, Pablo Escobar. It's such a misperception. The current reality of this city is so far removed from all that."

My host for the evening had just toured me around central Medellín, taking me to see apartment buildings that he was rehabbing and converting into rentals, including one in a neighborhood I'd not visited before. "Manhattan retro chic" might be the best way to describe it. Running off a carefully maintained, beautifully landscaped park, these few side streets are lined with small colonial structures housing sushi restaurants, funky bars, contemporary art galleries, and vintage clothing and furniture shops. The last thing I felt was unsafe.

As in Panama years ago, the opportunity today in Medellín is for the investor and the speculator. Prices are an absolute global bargain. Costs of getting in are low, and demand is expanding. Right now in this city you could buy almost anything and feel comfortable that you could make money from the purchase. And this is a market where you could buy even with very little capital, say $50,000.

The coming opportunity in Medellín is for the retiree. I predict that, five, seven years from now, when you say 'Medellín' to the average American, he'll think: retirement. Because that's what this City of Eternal Springtime is on track to offer—a very appealing and competitive retire-ment option.

Cautions associated with buying in Colombia have to do with exchange controls and other bureaucratic restrictions. Also, taxes are high. As an early investor or retiree in this country, you need to be prepared to navigate the system a little.

Croatia

Neckties and wine. Croatia may be better known for its long coast along the sparkling green Adriatic and its tumultuous, 1,000-year-long history, but when I think of Croatia, I think of neckties and wine. This gorgeous, complicated country is the birthplace of both the necktie and the Zinfandel grape, and these two facts reveal a lot about Croatia. First, it has great weather. The Zinfandel grape requires a climate not too hot and not too cold. Croatia's mild winters and sunny summers make for perfect Zinfandel grape growing.

Second, Croats are the trendsetters credited with introducing today's tie to the fashion world. The Croat contingent of the French service wore their traditional knotted handkerchiefs during the Thirty Years War (1618–1648). The Parisians took a fancy to them and called them *cravat*—a cross between the Croatian and French words for Croat (Hrvati and Croates). And thus a *cravat* fashion frenzy began. In the seventeenth century, these kerchiefs became so intricate that they were tied in place by strings and arranged in a bow that took forever to arrange.

Croatia is tucked into southeastern Europe, bordering the Adriatic Sea, between Bosnia, Herzegovina, and Slovenia. It's near the coast, Vienna, Venice, Budapest, skiing in Austria, and golf in Slovenia. It's been more than 20 years since the Socialist Federal Republic of Yugoslavia was dissolved. Its six republics—Croatia, Bosnia and Herzegovina, Macedonia, Montenegro, Serbia, and Slovenia—are all very much their own countries today. Croatia is wearing its new skin comfortably, as it should. The Kingdom of Croatia was, in fact, established in 925 CE. It joined Hungary in 1102 but maintained a Croat culture with hopes for independence. Although it was titled a free royal town in 1242, it took about 800 years before Croatia was independent again, this time from Austria-Hungary in 1918. That freedom, too, was short-lived, however. Croatia became part of Yugoslavia after World War II and didn't stand on its own again until 1992. A Croatian friend told me a story about his family once. "My father lived to be more than 100 years old," Lovorko explained. "He lived his whole life in Croatia, here in Istria—not only in the same town where he'd been born but in the same house. And, in his lifetime, he lived in nine different countries."

You have two strong lifestyle options in Croatia—the coast and the Istrian Peninsula. The Adriatic waters offshore from Croatia are a sailor's paradise. Inland, in Istria, is a wonderland of another kind, with vineyards and olive groves. If you've any romance in your soul, I defy you not to fall in love with this country. The ancient Romans called it Terra Magica, the Magic Land. Perhaps the best part is that, unlike Tuscany, the region of Italy that Istria is most often compared with (with good reason, as the geography and the history of these two regions have much in common), the average person can afford Istria, where you can buy a small, renovated cottage with lookouts over a valley and vineyards, perfect for regular visits, for rental, and for retirement, for as little as $100,000.

Retiring to Croatia, you'd be in good company. Diocletian, the only Roman emperor to abdicate his position (that is, to retire) was also the first person to retire overseas. Diocletian built a palace on the Dalmatian coast (his birthplace was Dalmatia), the location of current-day Split, and it is here, with the glorious Adriatic Sea spread out before him, that he chose to live out his days.

Dominican Republic

The Dominican Republic is an internationally popular all-inclusive resort destination that sees large numbers of tourists every year, thanks to its miles of sandy beaches and balmy temperatures. It's also, though, a top Caribbean choice for the would-be foreign property investor and retiree. All that tourist infrastructure amounts to an extensive network of businesses and services that the expat can easily plug into. As a property owner or retiree on this island, you have many more choices for the kinds of amenities you might be looking for than you'll typically find elsewhere in this part of the world.

Expats have been coming to the Dominican Republic, starting businesses and launching services geared toward their fellow foreign residents, for three decades. In the Samana Peninsula, for example, on the Dominican Republic's northeast coast, French and Italian food brands line the shelves of the expat-run specialty grocery stores, and signs for businesses are in English, French, Italian, and Spanish. Foreigners do not get curious looks, because there are so many of them. The locals have enjoyed friendly relations with these settlers for a long time.

The town of Las Terenas boasts the country's first drive-through bar and restaurant, owned and operated by a U.S. expat. Yes, drive-through bar. You pull up and order a cheeseburger and a beer to go. Your lunch is delivered to you in your car, and you continue on your way. When a need or market niche appears, an expat steps up to open a business to fill it. U.S., Canadian, French, and Italian expats run hotels, restaurants, cafés, and real estate offices throughout the country. A French doctor opened a medical practice to treat the thousands of French-speaking expats on the island. This is an entrepreneur's playground and a tax haven. As a foreign resident in the Dominican Republic, you pay no tax on money earned outside the country, not even on money remitted to the country for your living expenses.

Not every potential expat would be happy in this tourism-based culture, but life in the Dominican Republic has a great deal to recommend it, including its low cost. This is one of the most affordable lifestyle choices in the Caribbean, and the cost of real estate can be a tremendous bargain, as this country was hit hard by the downturn of 2008–2009. Property values are way, way down, construction companies have laid off workers, and real estate agencies have closed their doors. If you are a buyer with cash, you can almost name your price.

What could you buy? How about a brand-new, one-bedroom apartment about a 5-minute walk from a Caribbean beach for $100,000 or less. You can also find multimillion-dollar properties, and again, these are a bargain, compared with the cost of similar properties in other Caribbean markets.

Punta Cana is the Dominican Republic's most developed resort area. Puerto Plata, on the north coast, is probably the most developed area for both tourists and retirees. Most appealing, though, I'd say, is the Samana Peninsula. Here you have thousands of expats onshore and, in the water off the coast here, thousands of breeding humpback whales. It's a unique spot. It's also a little off the beaten path. You have to fly from the capital of Santo Domingo or drive the toll road, which is beautiful but takes about 2 hours.

The Dominican Republic is easily accessible, especially from the east coast of the United States. Gaining full-time legal foreign residency is a straight-forward proposition. You simply apply for provisional residency and then deposit the equivalent of $15,000 in a Dominican bank. After one year, you are granted full residency.

On the other hand, despite the established expat communities and the products and services they provide, this is a Third World country with Third World problems. It's also a Caribbean island in the hurricane zone.

Ecuador

Lots of overseas retirement destinations tout the fact that they're just like the United States, meaning that if you retired there, you could settle into familiar surroundings. You won't hear that about Ecuador. Each day you spend in this country, you know you're in a different and wonderful part of the planet.

Ecuador is also the world's best place to retire overseas on a budget and to live better for less. The cost of living is low, and the cost of real estate is near rock bottom for Latin America. The health care is high quality, honest, and inexpensive. Specifically, I would recommend Cuenca, Ecuador, a beautiful colonial city with a fresh, spring-like climate 12 months of the year and a large and growing expat community that is one of Latin America's most diverse and well blended.

Cuenca's historic center measures roughly 12 by 20 blocks, big enough but manageable. Most of the streets are of cobblestone and hemmed in by Spanish colonial buildings that seldom exceed three stories. Downtown Cuenca is generally well preserved, considering the original adobe construction, and today's Cuenca boasts cafés, restaurants, bars, and bookshops alongside traditional butchers, tailors, repair shops, clothing stores, and bakeries. The city is built around its beautiful town square, anchored by the original cathedral at one end (built in 1557) and the "new" cathedral (1800s) at the other. Ecuador has other colonial cities, but Cuenca is the cultural heart of the country, with an orchestra and active art, theater, even tango traditions that you can often enjoy for free.

Perhaps the biggest draw to Cuenca is its cost of living, which is low in an absolute sense. The falling dollar has caused prices to go up sharply for overseas Americans in many countries where goods are priced in the local currency. This won't happen in Ecuador as long as the country continues to use the U.S. dollar as its currency. Real estate, too, is an absolute bargain. You can buy a small condo for less than $40,000. The city's premium location is the historic center; this is the area that should hold its value even in the face of market ups and downs. It's a recognized world treasure.

To help with comparisons, note that the cost of a resale condo in Cuenca is about $800 to $900 per square meter. This number should get your attention. It compares with $1,200 to $1,500 per square meter for central Medellín, Colombia; with $1,500 to $1,800 for central Panama City; and with $1,800 to $2,000 per square meter for central Montevideo, Uruguay.

Although Cuenca is a developed city, much of Ecuador is not, with poor though improving infrastructure. Ecuador has the highest population density in South America (about 58 people per square kilometer) with a high percentage of indigenous and mestizos. This means we gringos stand out. If you want to blend in with the locals, you'd be more comfortable in another destination.

France

France has a polarizing effect on Americans. We either love the place or we hate it, and many of us believe the French hate us right back. That last part is wholly untrue in my experience. It's also not true that the French are rude. They're among the most well-mannered people I've come across anywhere.

Whenever readers of my e-letters ask for my recommendation for the best place in the world to live or retire, budget considerations notwithstanding, I recommend France. It's the world's best example, I believe, of getting what you pay for. There are reasons that France sees more tourists than any other country in the world, almost 80 million of them annually, which is a 20 percent larger number than the country's own permanent population. To accommodate all those tourists, the infrastructure of this country, from the airports to the train system, from the restaurants to the hotels, has to be top notch and it is.

France is not only perhaps the best place in the world to live, thanks to its food, wine, architecture, history, museums, parks, gardens, and cultural and recreational offerings, but it's also, thanks to its reliable tourist trade, one of the best places to think about parking some capital. A rental property in France, especially in Paris but elsewhere in the country, too, is about as recession-proof a real estate investment as you're going to find.

France would never feature on a list of the world's bargain destinations; still, outside Paris, this country can be more affordable than you might imagine and even Paris doesn't have to be hyperexpensive. Much of the best it has to offer comes free. But France isn't about cost of living; it's about quality of life. Paris is the most beautiful and romantic place on Earth, and France has much to offer beyond its City of Light. It can be possible to own your own piece of French country life for less than $100,000 (especially if you're up for a renovation project).

Downsides to France include the bureaucracy. Thanks to Napoleon, all Civil Law countries love their paperwork, but as ground zero for the Napoleonic Code, the French are best at this game. You can get almost anything done in this country if you have a paper stamped by some government official saying it's okay. It's getting that stamp that can leave you panting and ranting.

Ireland

Lief and I arrived on the Emerald Isle with our little family and our business expecting to plug into the kind of infrastructure we were used to back in the States. That didn't happen because the kind of infrastructure that we take for granted in the States (to do with transportation, telecommunications, banking, credit, etc.) doesn't exist in Ireland. Trying to run a business in this country, we felt like we were continually banging our heads against a collective Irish stone wall. Finally, frustrated and confused, we had to admit that we weren't going to change how the Irish lived and did business. We'd have to go along, and we did. Begrudgingly.

Now, years later, I find myself increasingly homesick for this country. With age and time, my perspective has shifted.

One day, after we'd been living in Waterford for maybe three years, a couple of readers stopped by our office. They were Indians, in the country to investigate the possibilities for relocating their software company from India to Ireland. They wanted to know if I had any advice for them. The couple represented the contradiction of the day. The Celtic Tiger was roaring loud, attracting investors (like us) from far and wide, entrepreneurs and business-people looking for opportunity, but we were all misguided. Ireland was holding out great opportunity, but not of the kind we were in the market for at the time, and that young Indian couple was confused when I warned them away. "Don't come to Ireland to run a business," I told them. "You'll be driven mad."

I'd stand by that advice today, but I'd add that that advice misses the point. We lived in this country during the apex of the Celtic Tiger, which generated great amounts of wealth, more money than this island had ever known. As a result, the Irish then, like us, were distracted from what was right in front of them. They were busy covering their ancient green land with suburban tract homes, shopping malls, and fast-food franchises. We watched as pubs were replaced by nightclubs and as car dealerships eventually kept Saturday business hours and banks finally remained open through lunch. Ireland wanted so badly to compete on the global business stage. In that regard, it failed completely.

But now, when I think of our time in Waterford, the things that come to mind have nothing to do with business. I remember the owner of the corner shop across the street from our office and how he and his wife sent us a small gift when Jack was born and inquired after both Jack and his big sister, Kaitlin, every time we saw them. I remember the cabinetmaker who helped to restore our big old Georgian house to its original glories, shutter by shutter, wood plank by wood plank. I think of the castles and the gardens we explored on weekends. I think of the few times we braved the beaches at Tramore, sitting on the sand in sweaters, shivering and shaking our heads, while out in the cold Irish Sea, the Irish swam and surfed. I think of cows blocking the roads and of sheep dotting the green fields. These are the pictures of Ireland I carry with me now.

By the time we left, Ireland had gotten very expensive. Today it's more affordable than it has been in more than a decade, its property market on par, more or less, with where it stood when we arrived 15 years ago. As a result, this country makes more sense as a place to think about living and investing than it has in a long time.

The surest bets for real estate purchase are the tourist trails—the Ring of Kerry, the southwest coast, Galway, and Dublin. Pay attention to proximity to amenities that are important to you—the ocean, a nearby airport so that you can hop around Europe, or a town so that you can walk where you want to go rather than driving (remember they drive on the left).

Italy

BARGAIN! Independent house, 130 square meters on two floors, composed of living room with fireplace, large kitchen, two bedrooms, bathroom. Private garden of 2,000 square meters. Good condition, recently restored. 75,000 euro.

That's a recent listing for a house in Italy. Not in Tuscany or Umbria but a corner of Italy that I'd say is at least as lovely. The beaches are golden, and the sea rolls out like a giant bolt of turquoise silk. Stitching together seascapes with lush mountain valleys, this region is one of Italy's secret treasures. You can have the best of all worlds here at prices a fraction of those in this country's more discovered regions. If your budget is small, you can still afford Italy, if you opt for Abruzzo. Real estate here is up to 80 percent cheaper than in Tuscany and up to 50 percent cheaper than in Umbria.

You know the appeals of Italy, but you may not realize the diversity of lifestyles on offer in this country. On my most recent visit to Italy, with Lief and the kids, we made a stab at recreating a version of the Grand Tour of old, exploring Italy's most heralded destinations with an eye to answering the question in each case, would we want to buy real estate or live here?

Venice is a gem of a place that you should see if you can. To be happy living here, you'd have to enjoy life on the water (getting anywhere requires a ferry or boat ride). I'd find it a hassle after a while. Certainly you'd want to leave in summer, when the temperatures can top 35 degrees Celsius for days on end and the narrow streets of this lagoon city are overrun with camera-toting hordes. In winter, the tourists are mostly gone, but the days are cold and damp. The real reason, though, why Venice isn't a top choice is its cost of living. Real estate values can exceed those of Paris (4,000 euro per square meter out-of-the-way to 20,000 euro per square meter overlooking the Grand Canal).

Ravenna is a stark contrast. This is a quiet Italian village with a rich history that today is largely overlooked. We made a point of stopping here because our art historian daughter wanted to see Justinian's mosaic in the Basilica of San Vitale. While in Venice, the queue for the basilica was hours long; in Ravenna, we walked straight up to the window, bought our tickets, and continued directly into the church, where we had no competition at all for front-row viewing of the ancient masterpiece. The heart of Ravenna's old town is interesting and pleasant but small. Overall, that's the trouble with this city—too small. What would you do here after you'd viewed the noteworthy art and architecture? On the other hand, lunch in Ravenna cost less than 10 euro per head, whereas the best you'll do in Venice will be more than double that.

Rome isn't small, and living here, you'd never run out of fun and interesting ways to spend your time. On the other hand, Rome is urban without the veneer that Paris has managed to paint over itself. Whereas Paris (to continue the comparison) is genteel and romantic, Rome is gritty and real. That said, Rome could be a much more affordable place to live than Paris. Avoid the tourist zones (as you would as a resident), and you could enjoy a full life here on an average budget.

One of Italy's biggest surprises is Pisa. Everyone comes to see the tower, but Pisa offers more. Its riverfront homes, candy-striped basilica, and baptistery showcase a bygone age of wealth. At one time, Pisa merchants competed successfully with those of Venice. Eventually, the city fell to Florence. Today, it's a 1-hour stop for tour buses, but if you're looking for an Old World lifestyle, I'd give this city more attention. The old town is charming, and the town beyond is pleasant. There's enough here to keep your interest and to support a fully appointed life on the Continent, and you're minutes from the sea. Whereas Venice, Rome, and Florence are given over entirely to tourists each season, Pisa is quiet year-round. Busloads of travelers come and go from the tower each day while the rest of the city goes about its business. Because few seem to recognize any reason to stick around, real estate can be a bargain. You could buy a one-bedroom apartment here for as little as $200,000.

If you're an art lover, Florence may seem like heaven, and, indeed, there's much in Florence to keep you occupied and engaged, but to me it doesn't feel like a place to call home. Whereas Pisa is cozy, Florence is aloof. Florence would also be a dramatically more expensive choice. Better, maybe, to base yourself in Pisa and visit Michelangelo's hometown. It's but an hour away via *autostrade*.

Malaysia

Showing the bias of my perspective, I refer to Malaysia as Asia's Panama. That is to say, this country is a regional and a global hub, for trade, for business, and for cultures. The cost of living is affordable, although elsewhere in Asia (Thailand, Vietnam, China) can be cheaper. Kuala Lumpur (KL), Malaysia's capital, is clean, efficient, and well functioning, with shopping, restaurants, and all the other trappings of a modern metropolis. It's also (again like Panama) an expat melting pot with big numbers of expats both from all over Asia and, to a lesser extent, the West. Malaysia is more welcoming of foreigners than any other country in Asia. Its My Second Home program makes retiree residency easy to obtain, meaning you don't have to worry about regular border runs, as many expats in this part of the world do. Because it is a former British colony, English is widely spoken, so you don't have to worry about trying to learn to speak Malay either.

Kuala Lumpur, located in the heart of the Malaysian peninsula, is a city of contrasts. The shining stainless steel Petronas Towers, two of the tallest skyscrapers in the world, anchor a startlingly beautiful and unique skyline. Modern, air-conditioned malls flourish, selling everything from batik clothing to genuine Rolex watches and Tiffany jewelry. In the shadows of these ultramodern buildings, the ancient Malay village of Kampung Baru still thrives, with free-roaming roosters and a slow pace of life generally found in rural villages. Less than a 20-minute walk from the city center, you can find yourself in the company of monkeys.

Life is different here than in the West. When you go to your neighborhood shop, take your time and converse with the owner, ask about his family as he asks you about yours. By the second or third time you visit, you are recognized and waved to when you walk down the sidewalk. You may be invited to dinner or at least to share a cup of rich *kopi*. In some Asian cities, it's easy for a foreigner to feel something akin to a walking wallet. Not in KL. Foreigners pay the same prices as the locals. Health care is first rate, public transportation is modern and efficient, and the tap water is safe to drink. Beautiful beaches are just a short drive or flight away, cool mountain retreats can be reached in less than an hour, and the thriving city-state of Singapore is easily accessible in a few hours by car, train, or bus or an hour by plane.

Although KL is more expensive than rural Malaysia, it is marvelously inexpensive by Western standards. You could realistically expect to cut your living expenses by a third and still enjoy a lifestyle comparable to what you are accustomed to now. If Asia interests you, this is one place where you could pursue the ultimate diversification strategy. That is, although Malaysia, like all of Asia, imposes restrictions on foreign ownership of land, you could purchase a house or an apartment in this country that could work for personal use, retirement, and rental. This is why Malaysia is one of but two Asian destinations I've chosen to highlight (the other is the Philippines, discussed later in this chapter).

Mexico

Mexico is a big place with a bad reputation. The reputation isn't altogether undeserved, as drug cartels do control parts of this country but not all of it, and some of the most appealing regions for both living and investing are outside the war zones. Mexico offers two long coasts, mountain towns, and colonial cities, plus Mayan ruins, jungle, rain forest, rivers, and lakes. It's also the most accessible overseas haven from the United States. You could drive back and forth if you wanted.

For all these reasons, Mexico is home to the biggest established populations of American expats in the world, making it a great choice if you seek adventure with the comforts of home. Mexico is no longer a supercheap option, but it is my top pick for enjoying a luxury coastal lifestyle on a budget, in Puerto Vallarta. Puerto Vallarta is more expensive than other places where you might consider living or retiring overseas, but in Puerto Vallarta that's not the point. This isn't developing-world living. This stretch of Mexico's Pacific coastline has already been developed to a high level. Life here can be not only comfortable but easy and fully appointed. In Puerto Vallarta, you aren't buying for someday, as you can be in many coastal destinations in Central America. In Puerto Vallarta, you can buy a world-class lifestyle in a region with world-class beaches and ocean views that is supported, right now, by world-class golf courses, marinas, restaurants, and shopping. This is a lifestyle that is available only on a limited basis worldwide, a lifestyle that is truly (not metaphorically) comparable to the best you could enjoy in southern California if you could afford it. Here you can afford it even on an average budget.

Real estate options in Puerto Vallarta vary from modest to jet-set, in terms of both products available and price points. You could buy a small apartment outside the town of Puerto Vallarta for less than $100,000, or you could buy big and fancy for $1 million-plus. Whatever you buy, you could rent it out when you're not using it. The Puerto Vallarta region, including the emerging Riviera Nayarit that runs north from it along the coast, is a tourist rental market with a track record.

The other spot in Mexico worth highlighting is Ajijic and Lake Chapala, in the mountains, one of the largest and most established expatriate communities in the world. Ajijic, less than an hour from Guadalajara, has been attracting retirees for decades thanks to its lake (despite the lake's on-and-off environmental problems) and cool weather. Again, you could buy here, small and modest, for less than $100,000.

New Zealand

New Zealand is the world's best place to escape the world. Safe, secure, and remote, this country is one of my top picks for part-time retirement overseas. It's not easy to arrange full-time legal residency in New Zealand and the country isn't interested in attracting the world's retirees, but you'll have no problem spending up to six months a year in this beautiful, English-speaking island nation. Six months in New Zealand and six months in the highlands of Mexico, for example, translates to perpetual summer.

New Zealand is one of the world's premier outdoor playgrounds, clean and green, with top-notch skiing, hiking, surfing, and fishing. The country is sometimes called the Ireland of the south; the landscapes are similar, as are the people. New Zealand's climate, though, is better. You could enjoy four real seasons on South Island.

A top living and investing choice on South Island is this country's garden city, Christchurch, with showcase botanic gardens, public parks, and nature reserves, as well as community vegetable plots, school planting projects, and well-kept private grounds. The gardens give this city lots of breathing space and provide a backdrop to its many festivals. With a population of only 370,000, Christchurch is a small city by world standards, but it is

New Zealand's second largest and offers all city amenities, from shopping, dining, and education to health care, entertainment, and recreational facilities. Lakes, rivers, wine country, beaches, ski fields, mountains, and thermal springs are all on the doorstep.

Because it is an English-speaking country, there are no obvious hubs for English-speaking expats. Christchurch, Riccarton, Upper Riccarton, and Avonhead attract Asian communities, with shops, hairdressers, and restaurants offering their services in Chinese and Korean languages. Fendalton, Merivale, and Strowan are more sought-after areas, with the city's biggest, nicest, and most expensive homes. (To put this in perspective, the average home in Christchurch sells for about $300,000, depending on the exchange rate.) Cashmere is Christchurch's most attractive hill suburb with the best views.

Other hill and beach suburbs were badly affected by the 2010 and 2011 earthquakes and are no longer as attractive as they once were. It is a testament to the city and its people that, in the aftermaths of these events, electricity was restored within hours in some areas, garbage was collected the next day, and the local newspaper was published and delivered. Places without water and sewage were provided with water tankers and chemical toilets. Still, these earthquakes were massive disasters. Many people are still suffering with poor quality roads, unemployment, and the loss of their homes, and many of the heritage buildings that made Christchurch famous have been lost. The prime minister has claimed that Christchurch, as it works to rebuild itself, will be the most livable city in New Zealand within the next 5 to 10 years. A new hub for technology and science is under way, and the general plan for reconstruction is a "city in a garden/garden in a city," with more green spaces and small squares.

Nicaragua

Nicaragua was once the breadbasket of Central America. Thanks to the first round of Sandinista rule and the confiscation of farmland in the name of "the people," that changed in the 1980s. The activities of the Sandinistas also created a stigma related to property rights in this country that remains. The country's current president, Sandinista Daniel Ortega, however, hasn't done anything to infringe on anyone's property rights. Still, since Ortega's reelection in 2007, foreign investors have stayed away from this market. The tourist trade continues, though, as Nicaragua, one of the lowest-cost destinations in Central America, continues to attract more than its share of backpackers and surfers.

Geographically, Nicaragua is blessed, with two long coastlines and two big lakes, plus volcanoes, highlands, rain forest, and rivers. In this regard, it's got everything Costa Rica and Panama have got, all less discovered and developed and available for the adventurer and eco-traveler at bargain rates. Architecturally, too, Nicaragua is notable. Its two sister colonial cities, Granada and León, vie for the title of Oldest City in the Americas. Whichever story you believe (that the Spanish conquistadores settled first on the shores of Lake Nicaragua at Granada or, perhaps, a few months earlier in Old León), Nicaragua is the big winner, with impressive colonial-era churches, public buildings, and parks to her credit.

Property values have fallen significantly in this country over the past several years, thanks to Ortega's reelection and then the global recession. As a result, you can buy a house on Nicaragua's Pacific coast for less than $100,000.

Panama

Panama has been one of the world's most important crossroads since the days when pirates ruled these waters. You name it; it passes through Panama in some way at some time going somewhere. Largely as a result of its crossroads positioning but also thanks to its reputation worldwide as a top retirement, tax, and business haven, Panama is the fastest-growing market in the region and one of the fastest-growing countries in the world.

Panama's benefits are many, including First World health care at Third World prices and the world's gold standard program of special benefits for retirees (plus 14 resident visa options for the nonretiree). It's also one of the world's few remaining tax havens (meaning you can operate an online business here tax free), and a U.S. dollar–based economy (meaning zero currency risk for dollar holders).

When the United States handed over Panama Canal operations to the Panamanians and the 10,000 U.S. military and their families departed the Canal Zone in 1999, the country fell into recession. A lot of disposable income disappeared overnight. Panama worked quickly to find ways to replace the lost economic activity. One focus since then has been to attract foreign retirees. In addition, the country has developed its tourism, banking, and financial services industries and is investing in the expansion of its canal with the expectation of generating more than $1 billion in profits annually after the expansion is complete.

Panama is a small country but offers many lifestyle and investment options, some better than others. Panama City is overpriced and overhyped, but if you work at it, you can still purchase an apartment in this city that will generate reliable cash flow and likely appreciate in value over the coming few years. Certainly you should be able to resell it easily when you're ready, as this is an active marketplace. The best buy outside the capital is Pacific beachfront. The farther from Panama City, the better the price.

Philippines

The Philippine Islands lie about 800 kilometers off the southeast coast of China and to the northeast of Borneo. More than 7,000 islands originating from volcanic activity form the archipelago, yet the total land mass is about the size of the state of Arizona. Only about 7 percent of the islands are larger than 1 square mile, and only one-third of the islands have names. Manila, the capital of the Philippines, is the largest city, with a population of over 10 million in the greater metro area and 1.5 million people in the city proper. Cebu City, the second-biggest city in the Philippines, has nearly 1 million residents. There are nearly 100 million in the country overall. The climate in the Philippines is tropical—that is, hot and humid. If that doesn't appeal to you, you should take the Philippines off your list.

The reason to consider this island nation is its cost of living and real estate. The Philippines is a popular destination among retired U.S. military people, because the local people are friendly, the health care is good, and a military pension buys a better-than-comfortable standard of living. As throughout Asia, foreign ownership of real estate is restricted, but you can buy a condo in your own name for full- or part-time use, retirement, and rental. The government seems to be on a path to relaxing foreign ownership restrictions.

I wouldn't recommend Manila. Too hot and too crowded. Instead, consider Cebu, which is protected by outer lying islands from the fierce typhoon winds that beat on some parts of these islands in most years. Winter in Cebu (October through February) can be delightful; temperatures are about 75 degrees Fahrenheit and accompanied by gentle breezes.

Expats in Cebu come from all over the world, but the majority are from the United States, England, and Australia, plus a few from Germany, including substantial numbers of men aged 45 to their mid-60s who've come so their pensions will stretch much further than they would back home and, often, to restart their lives with new wives and new families.

Romania

Romania's history dates back before the Roman Empire, but it's the conquest by the Romans that gave the region and the people their names. It also gave them their language, which is Latin-based and relatively easy for Westerners to decipher (unlike the languages of Croatia and Montenegro, for example). Thanks to its location, Romania has been in the middle of many of the great conflicts of the ages. The Goths, Huns, Magyars, Ottomans, and Austro-Hungarians all ruled over parts of Romania throughout the centuries. After World War II, the country fell under the influence of the Soviet Union.

Behind the Iron Curtain were centuries of history, the most famous of which became Dracula. Vlad the Impaler was actually a prince of Wallachia, the southern of the three principalities that became Romania. With castles and forests, rivers and mountains, and the Black Sea to the east, Romania has many stories to tell.

It also has vast resources and a central location that has allowed it to surge ahead economically after emerging from communism. Real estate prices saw big increases from 2004 to 2008 thanks to a rapidly growing middle class. Since 2008, Romania's real estate market has faltered, but it hasn't collapsed. In Bucharest, the capital, both new construction and the renovation of older buildings continues. Note that the older buildings can come with ownership and squatter complications.

Other things to watch out for in Bucharest are the red dot buildings. This city sits on a strong seismic fault line. The earth quakes regularly. The red dot buildings are those that have been identified as having structural damage from past quakes. Avoid them.

Romania's economy is being bolstered by new manufacturing plants, agriculture (including an expanding wine industry), and a slowly increasing tourist trade. Travelers come for inexpensive skiing in winter and the Black Sea coast in summer.

Bucharest is crowded and polluted with chaotic traffic and, again, earthquakes. Look instead to the mountains—specifically Brasov, Cluj, and Constanta. Winters can be bitter, but summers are ideal, and real estate prices are lower than in Bucharest, where they're a bargain.

Romania is a big Central European country that makes big sense right now for big, central production. Its port on the Black Sea gives access to the East and the Middle East, and more and more organizations worldwide are looking for ways to take advantage of this, including the U.S. Air Force, which is moving out of Germany and Turkey and into strategically located Romania. I don't know if this is a plus or a minus long term, whether for Romania or its residents or investors, but I remember that the U.S. military presence in Panama, for example, while it continued, proved a boon for that country's economy.

Spain

If culture is a priority for you, look to Spain. History, architecture, literature, art, and music are part of daily life. Outdoors enthusiasts, too, will enjoy Spain. The Spanish coast is a golfer's paradise. However, in many other regards, this is one of the most overhyped and disappointing stretches of coastline in the world. The nicest thing that can be said about it is that it's ultracheap in the wake of this country's ongoing property market collapse.

Spain has become a traditional retirement destination for Europeans, like Arizona and Florida for Americans. You can find here, if you're interested, big expat retiree communities along the Mediterranean coast and smaller ones elsewhere. Or you could decide on one of the country's interesting cities, from Barcelona to Valencia or Seville. If you prefer a cooler climate, look at the country's north coast.

One spot I would recommend is the Costa Tropical, one of the least-known, quietest, and most authentically Spanish of the Mediterranean *costas*. The Costa Tropical is in the province of Andalusia. It lies to the east of the infamous (and horrible) Costa del Sol and to the west of the desert-like Costa Almeria (spaghetti western country). The Costa Tropical's position between the brilliant blue Mediterranean and the soaring Sierra Nevada Mountains creates a subtropical climate where living things flourish. Attracting visitors for its climate, beaches, and scuba diving, it also makes a great base for exploring inland Andalusia and the beautifully preserved white villages of the Alpujarras, Granada's mesmerizing Alhambra Palace, and the Sierra Nevada National Park. Morocco is not far away.

Almuñécar (almoo-nyEAh-car), one of the Costa Tropical's three main communities, combines the charm of a typical Spanish town with the best of northern European influences and services. The locals are open and friendly, and the expats are happy to be here. This town, with a population of 22,000, has hung on to its Spanish charm, unlike the better-known Spanish coastal towns, and tends to attract more Spanish than foreign visitors. The town has an incredibly wide range of historical influences, including Phoenician, Roman, and Moorish. "How could you live anywhere else?" asks the town's mayor, Juan Carlos Benavides, and he may have a point.

Uruguay

Uruguay is known the world over for the beautiful beaches running the entire length of its coast. The country's best value in beach property is the Costa de Oro, a 30-mile stretch of shoreline with uninterrupted golden sands whose name translates to the "gold coast." What's more, the Costa de Oro also contains some of Uruguay's best coastal towns for full-time retirement living. It offers something else, too, that most of the Atlantic coastline does not: incredible sunsets, thanks to the general east-west orientation of its shoreline.

Best of all, you're in Uruguay, a country that offers a peaceful, genuinely laid-back culture, along with a notable absence from the world's conflicts, and where expats can obtain easy residency and even a second passport. Uruguay has a solid financial center and an economy that continued to grow during the recent worldwide recession. It's also a country with abundant groundwater, mild weather, and a surplus of renewable electricity from hydro power. All things considered, it is an appealing package—a beautiful coastline with First World infrastructure, a solid democracy with a healthy financial system, and shady seaside towns where the beachfront homes start at just $75,000.

Uruguay is located on lower South America's eastern seaboard, wedged between Argentina and Brazil. The country shares a land border with Brazil and is separated from Argentina by a wide river, the Río de la Plata. The capital city of Montevideo, the southernmost capital in the Western Hemisphere, is home to almost half of Uruguay's 3.3 million residents. Roughly the size of the American state of Missouri, Uruguay is the second-smallest country in South America after Suriname.

In the 1800s, the country's Costa de Oro was considered a worthless stretch of land. It consisted mostly of moving dunes, which in some places extended for miles inland from the sea. Two of the area's first development initiatives were dune forestation projects at Atlántida and La Floresta, resulting in today's abundance of shady pines, eucalyptus, and sycamore trees in these spots. By 1910, the area was starting to get the attention of Montevideo's wealthy families who were looking for country getaways and seaside retreats. In the late 1930s, development increased dramatically as the first land subdivisions were planned. The area drew the attention of European investors looking for a sound place to invest outside Europe as World War II began. This stretch of coastline continued to be popular, attracting the elite of Montevideo and beyond, until the 1950s. Then the Punta del Este began to draw wealthy vacationers farther along the coast. The Costa de Oro's popularity is on the upswing again, as expats and second-home shoppers from North America are taking note of the excellent property values on offer.

Uruguay can qualify as sleepy, which can be a pro or a con, but never-sleepy Buenos Aires is only a quick flight or ferry ride away. The other potential downside to this country is the distance from North America and the fact that few flights serve Montevideo direct from the United States. You have more options connecting through Buenos Aires.

You're Not in Kansas Anymore

Eight Unexpected Realities of Buying Real Estate Overseas and How to Prepare for Them

hile Lief and I began our overseas real estate investing careers unassumingly together in Waterford, Lief had made his first property investment before I knew him, in the States, and with a far more direct agenda: to make money. A few years before we met, Lief had taken a $5,000 gift and turned it into a $150,000 profit through a real estate deal in Ravenswood. Ravenswood is a north-side Chicago neighborhood of middle-class office workers and first-generation Latino immigrants, a very up-and-coming, working-class kind of place at the time. Here, after months of searching and negotiating to put together a deal that allowed him to make the buy with but $5,000 cash, Lief had invested in a building configured as three two-bedroom flats. He lived in one of the apartments and rented out the other two. The rents generated a good income from the start and for more than two years to follow. After that time (just 30 months later), Lief sold the property and walked away with $150,000 after expenses. Not a bad return on $5,000. It was that $150,000 that made it possible for us to purchase Lahardan House in Ireland. And it was the profits from Lahardan House that later made possible our purchase in Paris and so on, through more than three dozen purchases in 21 countries to date.

Lief is a bona fide start-from-next-to-nothing overseas property investor success story. It's important to note, though, that he couldn't have gotten his start, at least not in the way he did, negotiating a $200,000 investment with but $5,000 working capital, most anywhere but in the United States. As I've mentioned, that kind of real estate investing doesn't exist most anywhere else, because that kind of real estate investing depends on leverage. Historically, in the United States, it has been possible, at times, to borrow more than 100 percent of the purchase price for a piece of property and to negotiate terms allowing up to 30 years, for example, to pay back the borrowed amount at a very reasonable fixed rate of interest. Lief's financing on that Chicago building was a 98 percent loan-to-value (LTV) mortgage. As he intended to live in one of the units, it was considered a loan for an owner-occupied property and qualified for the high LTV. This is unheard of in most of the rest of the world.

10 Don't Count on Leverage

n much of the rest of the world, it is not possible for a foreign buyer to borrow money locally for the purchase of real estate, period. No bank will lend to you. In places where it is possible for a foreigner to borrow to buy, you won't find the terms as appealing as they can be stateside. In the final years of the real estate bubble in Ireland, banks in that country were offering 110 percent loan-to-value (LTV) financing. The extra 10 percent was to cover stamp duty (a tax charged of the buyer at the time of purchase in Ireland) and other closing costs. This very aggressive approach to mortgage lending was one of the factors contributing to the collapse of Ireland's banking industry. It goes without saying that you can't borrow 110 percent of the purchase price of a piece of property in Ireland today. In the current global climate, I don't know any bank in any country offering 110 percent LTV financing (although some banks in Spain will lend you 100 percent and maybe even 110 percent as a resident). Your financing options as a foreign buyer today are limited. Mortgage industries, in countries where they exist, are less sophisticated and less competitive than in the United States, meaning fewer products and less room for bargaining on the part of the borrower. In the wake of what the real estate investment world has witnessed over the past half-dozen years, they are also very conservative.

Specifically, outside the United States, fixed-rate mortgages are rare. Western Europe is one region where a foreigner can borrow locally for the purchase of real estate; however, no bank in this part of the world is going to offer you a 30-year loan at a fixed rate of interest. In some European countries, your options can include 5-year fixed and occasionally 10-year fixed rates on 20- or 25-year mortgages, but adjustable-rate loans are the norm. Furthermore, few banks in Europe are going to give a foreign borrower 30 years to pay back a loan (exceptions are some banks in France and Spain). Also note that some banks won't lend more than 50 percent LTV if the property is being purchased as a rental investment.

One cost to getting a mortgage overseas that you may not expect can be life insurance. Banks in most countries where you'll be able to borrow as a foreigner for the purchase of property are going to require you to take out a life insurance policy for the amount of the mortgage (usually a declining balance policy) naming the bank as beneficiary. Foreign banks don't want to worry about getting paid or foreclosing if you die. If you're buying for investment, this expense can cut into your return. If you're buying for retirement, this can amount to an even greater cost in the scheme of things, because life insurance is more expensive the older you get. In addition, the policy must be local, issued by a local agency, so any life insurance you may already have back home typically won't meet the requirement. Furthermore, in most countries, it's not possible to obtain life insurance to cover you beyond the age of 70 or 75. This means that if you're a 65-year-old borrower, you won't be able to qualify for even a 20-year mortgage. The best term you'll be able to negotiate would be for 5 or 10 years.

Finally note that, if you're obtaining a mortgage in the name of both you and your spouse, you'll need two life insurance policies, one for you and a second one for your spouse. On the other hand, the joint borrower concept can help you out if, instead of a spouse, you name one of your kids on the mortgage with you. Some banks will agree to use the younger borrower's age to set the loan period, even if this means your life insurance policy will expire before the term of the loan.

In markets where it's not possible to organize bank financing, one option is to negotiate terms with the seller, whether an individual owner or a developer. Developer financing is more common today in many countries than it has ever been, as developers in developing markets understand that Americans (one of their biggest pool of potential buyers) no longer have access to the ready cash they once had back home (in the form of a second mortgage or line of credit for real estate they own in the United States, for example). In Panama, Nicaragua, Belize, Uruguay, Colombia, Ecuador, Argentina, and beyond, both developers and private sellers, if they don't need the cash immediately themselves, are willing to allow you to stretch out payment over time. Typical seller terms might be as little as 50 percent down at closing and the remaining 50 percent due at regular intervals over, say, three, five, or seven years. In Panama today, it's not uncommon for sellers to suggest "creative" financing. If your seller doesn't bring it up, in Panama or wherever you're buying, you should. It won't hurt to ask.

Formal developer financing (that is, financing not negotiated on a one-off basis but available to all buyers from a developer) can require less in the way of a down payment, even (on rare occasions) zero down. Interest rates can be 5 to 15 percent, and a typical term for organized developer financing might be 10 years, with a balloon payment at that time. These kinds of developer financing opportunities can be very appealing, but you want to be sure you understand all the nuances and variables before signing the contract. Recent financing offered by developers at work on the north coast of Brazil is a good case study, showing the pluses and the minuses of this kind of leverage.

Another option to local financing for the purchase of real estate overseas can be to tap your IRA funds. Most custodians of these kinds of accounts don't allow for "nontraditional" types of investments such as foreign real estate. The important thing to understand is that it's not that you can't use your IRA funds to invest in real estate overseas. It can be, though, that your custodian doesn't want you to, either because he doesn't want (or under-stand how) to deal with the required paperwork or, more often, because he makes more money if you invest in one of his preferred investment products.

To buy real estate, foreign or local, with your retirement funds, you can set up what's called a self-directed IRA or self-directed 401(k). In theory, this means you're in a position to direct the investment of your account funds. However, you still must go through the custodian, asking him to make the investment for you. He can refuse. The best (in some cases, depending on what you want to do, the only) way, therefore, to take control of your IRA funds is to establish what I refer to as a checkbook IRA.

To do this, you set up an account with a self-directed IRA custodian. Then you create an LLC (I'd recommend an offshore LLC if your intention is to purchase foreign real estate), in which your IRA invests all its funds. Then you, as the president/manager of that LLC, invest the funds of your IRA as you like. This structure allows you to eliminate the paperwork (and the review process) otherwise required each time you invest in something alternative. You simply write a check from the LLC's bank account to make the purchase.

When investing with a self-directed IRA, remember the self-dealing rules. For example, and broadly speaking, you can't have your IRA buy real estate from you directly; you can't have your IRA invest in any business you own or operate; and you can't have your IRA buy a property and rent it out to your business. In addition, and importantly, note that you can't use your IRA self-directed funds to buy real estate for personal use; the property must be an investment. You can't buy a vacation home with IRA funds, for example, and then spend three months a year using it. However, you could buy a piece of real estate with the plan to rent it out until you retire. Then, once you do retire, you could take the property as a distribution from your IRA and move in. This can be a great strategy if you identify your potential retirement residence now but don't plan to retire for some time.

11 Don't Expect Comps

The other thing that doesn't exist in most of the world is comparables. "Running comps," as any would-be real estate buyer would do when shopping in the United States, depends on referencing a multiple listing service (MLS). No such organized, computerized, easily accessible database of properties on the market exists in most of the world. With limited exceptions, the MLS is a U.S. market phenomenon, an indispensable tool that, somehow, the rest of the world's real estate markets manage to survive without.

With an MLS, you can find out, within minutes, what every property of a certain type in a certain area has sold for within a certain period of time. Without an MLS, you can't. Take a minute to think through the implications. What should a two-bedroom, two-bath apartment of 2,000 square feet in a certain neighborhood in Panama City cost? Without an MLS to reference (and no MLS exists in Panama, although the local real estate industry is working to create one) to find out what every property fitting that description has sold for in the past year, say, you have no idea, and neither does anyone else. The owner of an apartment fitting that description can decide he'd like to sell it for whatever he'd like to sell it for, and who are you, or anyone, to tell him that his price isn't appropriate? You, he, and anyone else who might be interested have nothing to compare it to.

That's just the start of what it means to shop for real estate in a market without an MLS. It also means that every agent operating in that market has access to his listings only. No real estate agent in Panama City can tell you about every two-bedroom, two-bath, 2,000-square-foot apartment for sale in a particular area or neighborhood of the Panamanian capital, because he doesn't know about every apartment fitting that or any other description currently available. He knows only about the apartments his agency has listed. His listings are proprietary, as are the listings of every other agency in the market. To find out about every apartment of a certain description in a certain region, you've got to meet with many different real estate agents operating in that region.

When you do, you'll discover, probably, that some apartments fitting your criteria are listed with more than one agent. This is not because those agents are sharing the listing, but because the seller has listed his apartment with more than one agent, perhaps, you'll find, at different prices. Listings are proprietary but not necessarily exclusive.

Some foreign markets are more open in this context than others. In Panama City, for example, some agents will work together, allowing other agents to show their listings and, if a sale is made through another agent, splitting the commission. In other markets, such as the one in Ireland, agents are more cutthroat. When we were living in Waterford, there were eight or nine agencies operating in the city. Not only would an agent working at one agency not ever consider the idea of cooperating with an agent from another agency, he wouldn't even say hello to any competing agent he passed on the street.

Lief and I are currently shopping for a house to buy in Panama City. We have been viewing properties for almost a year. We're working with three agents. Each has taken us to see houses that the others may or may not have known were listed for sale but that, even if they knew of them, the other agents wouldn't have been able to show us. More than once, we've found a listing that one agent had shown us available from another agent at a different price. Bottom line, after almost 12 months of serious searching, I couldn't tell you what the house we want to buy should cost. We can't reference comps, because they don't exist. We can't find out how many houses of the kind we're shopping for have sold in the past year. We still have no idea, really, how active the market is for the kind of property we're hoping eventually to buy. All we can do is compile our own data, based on the pricing and specs of the properties we've viewed. We've seen a 2,500-square-foot house on a small lot in a not-ideal neighborhood priced for two times as much as a 4,000-square-foot house on a bigger lot in a better neighborhood.

Multiple listing services do exist in a few localized markets of Latin America, including on the Bay Island of Roatan off the coast of Honduras, in Buenos Aires, and in parts of Mexico, including Puerto Vallarta. Beyond those few regions, you must do your best to create your own database detailing properties, sizes, locations, and prices for your own reference.

12 Google Isn't Always Your Friend

Google is generally recognized today as the answer to every question, but there are exceptions to that Internet Age fundamental and one of them has to do with shopping for real estate overseas. As you launch your foreign property adventures, your first instinct may be to Google in some direction, to surf around online for country agents and property listings. I encourage you to resist that urge.

Well, that's overstating things. Go ahead and spend time online searching property-related keywords for the destinations that interest you. You can acquire background this way, gain a starter understanding of the geography, the neighborhoods, and the property options on offer wherever you're searching, and begin to identify price points. All of that can be helpful if you keep it in perspective. Whatever information you find online to do with the state of a market, with sample property listings or with current pricing, will be confused and confusing. Often it will be plain wrong, and when you think through what's going on, you'll understand why. In fact, several things are going on that keep the Internet from being your friend when it comes to finding a piece of property worth buying in another country.

The first has to do with language. Search online in English for information on real estate for sale anywhere in the world where the people don't speak it as a first language, and what are you going to find? If you find anything at all (in some small non–English-speaking markets, online representation in English may be nonexistent), it'll be information and listings from those involved with the property market in that place who do communicate in

English. Who might that include? Gringos. (If you're bothered by this description, see Chapter 14.)

We gringos have made big marks on some of the property markets in this part of the world, especially in Central America. Over the past three decades, we have been identifying particularly appealing pieces of this region, especially along its coastlines, buying them cheap, chopping them up into smaller pieces, repackaging them, and then reselling them, primarily to fellow gringos. We have created markets where none existed, reengineered off-the-map fishing villages into high-end holiday towns. Along the way, a lot of us gringos (and a lot of locals, too) have made a lot of money, and other gringos, with lifestyle, rather than investment agendas, have acquired reinvented retirements and second homes in the sun.

As a result, today, in many places throughout Latin America, especially in Central America, the gringo force is well established and strong, particularly in the context of the local property markets. In places like Ambergris Caye, Belize; Roatan, Honduras; Boquete, Panama; and Playa del Carmen, Mexico, more real estate is sold by gringo agents than any other kind. The last time I counted, the very small island of Roatan, in the Bay Islands off the Caribbean coast of Honduras, was home to more than a dozen gringo agencies and only one owned and operated by a local Honduran.

These agents may or may not be qualified, they may or may not have any previous experience selling real estate, they may or may not be trustworthy or reliable, but they all have one thing in common: They speak English as a first language. And this makes them feel safer to the rest of us who also speak English as a first language. We can understand them better than we can understand an agent stammering away at us in Spanglish, and so we assume, subconsciously, that they understand us, too. Critically, we also assume, subconsciously, if we let ourselves, that they have our best interests at heart. We're all in this together, right? We are English-speaking strangers in this strange land—surely we're all looking out for each other.

In some emerging markets where you might be considering investing in real estate, this couldn't be further from the Wild West reality you're going to face on the ground, including among (and especially among) the gringo real estate agents you'll encounter. The trouble is that, because they're able to communicate in English, these are the agents you're going to find when you carry out any English-language, property-related search online. Any English-language search is going to return information and listings published by agents who deal in English, and it's these agents who are most experienced and most savvy at taking advantage of foreign, and especially first-time foreign buyers.

You want to expand your search beyond these guys to include local agents. This requires local language skills. The best case is when you have them yourself, but if you don't, you have two options that can also be effective at making it possible to penetrate from the gringo to the local market. You can enlist help from a friend who speaks the local language, or you can engage someone specifically for that purpose, a translator. I have done both things successfully in markets around the world. If you're not working with a friend you know and trust, the key is finding someone you can come to know and trust. Don't advertise for an "English-Language Translator to Help a Foreigner with the Purchase of Property." Yikes—the characters that ad would attract! You find a property scout/property search translator in a foreign country the way you find most things in a foreign country, from a maid to a plumber, a doctor, or an attorney—by word of mouth. When entering any new market, make one connection you trust and then build out from there.

Language is perhaps the biggest reason why Google is not usually your friend when it comes to shopping for real estate in another country, but there are others, including the fact that once on Google, always on Google. Search online for property listings anywhere in the world, and what will you find? Current listings? Recent listings? Former listings? Old listings? Outdated listings? Sold listings?

Yes. And usually it's impossible to tell them all apart. Maybe an online search will lead you to agent contacts that ultimately prove worthwhile, but the particular listings it yields likely will not. And this occurs not only because chances are good that those listings will no longer be current by the time you find them, but also because chances are good they'll also be either misrepresented or posted with inflated price tags or both.

A reader of my daily e-letter contacted my Panama office staff a few years ago to say that she was interested in buying an apartment in Panama City. She'd been searching online for months and had finally found one she thought she wanted to move ahead with. Would we mind going to have a look at it for her, as she couldn't get to Panama anytime soon herself? Sure, we told her. My assistant called the agent and made an appointment to meet her at the apartment at lunchtime that afternoon. Marion printed out the listing from the agent's website to take with her. She returned an hour later shaking her head.

"There's no pool!" she exclaimed as she walked into my office.

"Excuse me?" I replied, not picking up on the reference.

"At the apartment I went to see for the reader who contacted us this morning. The listing online shows a beautiful pool and social area. After I'd toured the apartment, I asked to see the pool.

"'Oh, there's no pool with this building,' the agent responded.

"Do you know what she said? She told me, 'Oh, that pool's not in this building. It's at the hotel down the street.'

"Told me that just like it were the most normal thing in the world.

"The apartment is horrible," Marion continued. "Nothing like in the photos or the description online. But at least there is an apartment. There's no pool. No pool at all!"

That's an extreme example, but it's not uncommon for online listings to play fast and loose with reality.

13 Why *Net Pricing* Is a Dirty Word

A s I've explained, although, in most property markets around the world, listings are not shared, neither are they generally exclusive. Sellers can list with as many agents as they'd like, to improve their chances of selling. Because listings aren't shared and because, again, in most of the world, there's no such thing as a multiple listing service, it's easy for any agent who takes a listing to offer the property for whatever price she wants. Some set prices to include what most of us would recognize as reasonable commission rates. Others are more aggressive.

Here's how this can work: A seller tells an agent he wants $100,000 for his piece of property. The agent then, in many markets, can list the property for whatever price he'd like—say $150,000, to use a round number as an example—even though the standard commission in that market might be 7 or 8 percent, but certainly not 33 percent. The $50,000 difference is the net, and this approach to pricing is one reason why, in many developing markets, it's not uncommon to find the same piece of property listed for sale with different agencies at different prices.

Here's an example of how net pricing can work: A seller tells his cousin that he wants to sell his property for $50,000. The cousin tells his neighbor that the property is available and adds $5,000 to the price as commission for himself. The neighbor tells his brother and adds $10,000 for himself. Then the brother of the neighbor goes to a real estate agent, offering to place the property for sale with that agent and adding another $15,000 to the price as his take. Now, as far as the agent is concerned, the price of the property is

$80,000. He adds $20,000 for his own commission and begins promoting the listing. This example is the most common with raw land in the countryside, where the owner may not even know that the real estate agent listing his land in the city exists.

With no multiple listing service, no agency cooperation, and often no decent sales records, foreign real estate markets are studies in inefficiency. You can do your research to try to determine current prices and values, but your best defense against being the victim of net pricing is to deal direct with the seller to negotiate price. This doesn't eliminate the risk of being stung by net pricing, but it should reduce it.

Note that real estate agents don't have the monopoly on net pricing shenanigans. Years ago, a reader of my newsletter arranged to meet with my correspondent in Ecuador to get information about buying real estate in that country. The correspondent happened to live in the particular small town where this reader was interested in buying and was happy to meet over coffee. The reader and my correspondent discussed the pros and cons of the area, and the reader, convinced that this was the place for his retirement, asked for a local real estate agent recommendation. The correspondent obliged and took the reader to meet the agent he had used to buy his own apartment.

The reader met with the agent and then went on his way, saying he wanted to look around town a little on his own. While wandering around, the reader met a local kid on the street somewhere who spoke excellent English. The reader asked him if he knew about any houses for sale, thinking he'd get one over on the real estate agent by buying direct and eliminating the commission. The kid showed the guy a few houses, and, long story short, the reader ended up buying one.

After the closing, the reader contacted my correspondent to gloat over the great deal he had gotten on his house by not using the real estate agent. My correspondent explained that, alas, that same house had been listed with the agent he'd introduced to the reader for about 25 percent less than what the reader had paid.

Again, if at all possible, negotiate with the owner of the property you're interested in buying directly.

14

You're a Gringo— Get Over It

I don't use the term *gringo* pejoratively but as shorthand, as it is often used to refer to anyone in this part of the world who hails originally from North America or Europe. You can throw in Australians and New Zealanders, too. Considered collectively south of the Rio Grande, these folks—Americans, Canadians, Germans, Dutch, British, French, Aussies, Kiwis, and so on— count as gringos. Don't take any offense; usually none is intended.

Don't be bothered by being a gringo but don't forget that you are one, either. Recognize that this status can make you a target. It is commonly believed among the general population of Central America that all gringos are rich and therefore can afford to pay more for anything, from a hammock to a beachfront lot, than a local. When they see the color of our skin or hear the accent in our Spanish, they hike up the price.

In some parts of the world, land prices can be so low that even the gringo price will seem cheap. A colleague moved to Costa Rica several years ago and decided he wanted to invest in the local real estate market. The first year, he knew he was being quoted only gringo prices so he didn't buy anything but kept researching and scouting. The second year he thought he had penetrated to local-level pricing, because he was being quoted prices 20 percent lower than the year before (even though the market had appreciated nicely overall in the intervening months). He bought a few pieces of land and kept looking for more good deals.

In year three, my colleague engaged a local scout, who was quoted prices a further 20 percent below prices from year one (again, even though the market had continued to move up overall). In retrospect, my colleague now sees that it wasn't until year four that he in fact gained access to true local-level pricing. This is not to say that he didn't make good investments in his first couple of years of buying. Those buys have appreciated in value, but the best deals were made in year four and beyond.

15 Rights of Possession and Other Ownership Concerns

Do you think he'd take $10,000?"

"Yes, I'm pretty sure he'd jump at that."

"Would he take $8,500? At $8,500, I'd cash him out on the spot."

"Well, that'd be $1 a meter. He might go for it. Then you'd have money left to use to title the property if you decide you want to."

"Right, but maybe I won't worry about it. I'll fix the house up, and it'll be a great place to stay when we want to go fishing. If you really think I could get the place for $8,500, that'd be tremendous. Other places I've looked at that could work as a fishing getaway have been $200,000 and more."

"Yes, well, you need to understand. You can have problems with rights of possession property. You need to be careful. Still, $1 a meter . . . You can't beat that, there's not a lot of downside."

This conversation took place between two American guys sitting across a wood table from each other. They were whiling away another sunny afternoon in paradise, sipping local $1 beers beneath the shade of a thatched roof. I was a few feet away, swinging in a hammock. If they knew I was there, they didn't seem to mind, so I swung back and forth slowly, eavesdropping in silence.

In Panama, rights of possession (ROP) property can cost a fraction of what titled property would cost, but there's a reason for that. To say that you "can have problems with rights of possession" is understating the reality, because, although you can purchase rights of possession property, you don't own it. All you've bought is the right to possess the property. That doesn't make it yours. Treat it like it's yours—investing in improvements, building a house on it, making plans related to its long-term use—and you can have a shock one day when you show up after an absence to discover someone else living in your house, enjoying your improvements, and making his own plans related to the property's future.

Rights of possession land isn't uncommon in parts of Panama, specifically Bocas del Toro, for example. You need to understand the distinction between ROP and freehold title before you make a purchase, not only in Bocas, but anywhere in Panama. "I've learned my lesson," one frustrated gringo buyer told me years ago. "I just don't believe anyone, not any attorney, certainly not any real estate agent, who assures me that ROP's no problem. I know better. My attorney insisted all along, from the first day I notified him of my intended purchase, that I'd be able to have the property titled. I went through the titling process, filed all the paperwork, paid all the fees, then my application for title was returned with a big 'Denied!' stamp on the front. No reason that made any sense, simply denied.

"I went back to my attorney, who made further filings (and charged more fees), only again to be told that no, my ROP land couldn't be titled. I still don't really understand why, and now I have no idea what to do," the poor guy concluded.

Sometimes ROP land can be converted to titled property, meaning that an ROP purchase can be one of the best ways to buy for investment, because, as the gentleman sitting across from me that day I lay swinging quietly in my hammock in a local Panama hangout pointed out, the cost can be a fraction the cost of comparable titled land. Buy for $1 a meter, successfully convert the ROP to freehold title, and you can turn around and flip for many multiples of what you paid. The key is to be really, really sure you'll be able to convert the ROP to title. To make that determination with confidence, you need the counsel of an attorney who knows what he or she is talking about and who has experience dealing with ROP issues. As the American buyer I quote above discovered too late, this is not the case with all attorneys you might find in an area where ROP land is being sold.

When buying a piece of real estate in the United States, we take clean title for granted. We don't wonder whether the guy offering to sell us a house in fact owns the house. We don't ask the young man who takes us to see his uncle's beachfront lot whether the uncle knows that the kid is trying to sell off the old guy's land. It doesn't occur to us that a piece of real estate is being offered with anything but freehold title or that we need to investigate the history of ownership. When shopping for real estate overseas, you can't take any of those things for granted.

I got my first taste of how fuzzy things regarding the ownership of a piece of property, current and historic, can be in Nicaragua. The history of ownership of property in this country can be complicated. Land in Nicaragua can be *cooperativa,* Somoza, or agrarian reform. Bottom line, these descriptions translate as risky. Buy a piece of beachfront property once held by a *cooperativa,* and you run the risk that dozens of claimants could appear at some time in the future to dispute your ownership. Buy a piece of Somoza land, and the Nicaraguan government could someday lay claim to it.

When I began spending time in Nicaragua, I was scouting on my own account but also as a writer covering this beat. I began reporting on the title issues as I understood them, telling my readers that they couldn't take for granted that any piece of property they might be interested in buying in Nicaragua would transfer to them with clear and clean freehold title. Further, I advised, they couldn't believe every property agent who assured them that *cooperativa* land was the same as freehold title or that a Somoza title could be "cleaned up." Agents I met made these claims but had neither the intention nor the resources to back them up.

After I'd been reporting on this market for a couple of years, one of the real estate agents operating in Granada, Nicaragua, who I'd gotten to know well, stopped me in Granada's central square to say: "Kathleen, you've got to stop pushing this title thing. It's interfering with sales."

You've likely heard of the potential title complication in Mexico. It's referred to as *ejido* land. This is land the government gave to locals to farm. It's something akin to *cooperativa* land in Nicaragua, as it's owned by the community working it, not by any individual, and therefore isn't titled. *Ejido* land can be titled if the entire *ejido* votes to do so. As with rights of possession land in Panama, you want to have an *ejido* in Mexico title the land before you pay them for it. Most of the confiscated land stories that have come out of Mexico and were so well publicized by the U.S. media have had to do with *ejido* land. In most cases, a gringo developer "bought" from the *ejido* but never actually had the property titled. The Mexican government technically still owned it. When the Mexican government decided, in each case, to exercise its claim and take back the land from the *ejido* (as the *ejido* was no longer using it for the intended purpose of community farming), it wasn't doing anything wrong, and it certainly wasn't stealing land from the foreign "owners." The foreign owners weren't owners at all. In reality, they were squatters. Maybe they had been duped by the developer who sold to them. Maybe the developer didn't realize himself that he was selling land without title and that he, therefore, didn't in fact own.

Before we go further, we should address a common initial concern among would-be overseas property buyers—namely, can foreigners own property in another country? The general answer is yes, but there are exceptions, most commonly in Asia. Some countries in this part of the world do place heavy restrictions on or outright ban foreign ownership. Sometimes, in these countries, foreigners intent on owning find ways to work around the rules, with the help of local partners, for example. This is risky, and I don't recommend it.

However, in most countries where you might want to buy real estate, you can do so in some cases with certain restrictions. The most common restriction has to do with foreign ownership of land within so many kilometers of an international border or a coastline. In Mexico, for example, a foreigner can't own within 100 kilometers of an international border or within 50 kilometers of a coastline unless you hold the property in a *fideicomiso* (a trust). The government has allowed this trust workaround since 1993. Before then, foreigners had to hold property in those zones as leasehold.

The distance from an international border restriction varies by country. Panama has a 10-kilometer rule that is absolute, that is, no workaround allowed as it is in Mexico. Argentina imposes the restriction but only generally. No specific distance is stipulated, but you can figure that, as a foreign buyer, you're going to have to get government approval to buy anything within 50 kilometers of a border. Recently, Argentina also put in place restrictions pertaining to the amount of agricultural land that foreigners can own. The maximum number of allowable hectares per individual foreign owner is now 1,000, and the total amount of agricultural land owned by foreigners in Argentina can't exceed 15 percent of the country's total available agricultural land. Brazil has a similar rule, stipulating that no more than 2 percent of that country's agricultural land can be owned by foreigners. In Brazil, though, the rule is state by state (that is, no more than 2 percent of the agricultural land in each state can be held by foreigners).

Croatia imposes one of the most interesting foreign ownership restrictions I've come across. A foreigner can purchase property in Croatia if Croatians can own property in that foreigner's country. This gets interesting for us would-be American buyers. The United States imposes no foreign ownership restrictions on Croatians, so, in theory, we Americans should be able to buy without restriction in Croatia. However, Croatia, in making that determination, considers the United States not as a country but rather each individual state. If you're from Arkansas, Croatia is going to want to see documentation showing that Arkansas allows Croatians to own in that state. The fact that Arkansas places no restriction on Croatian ownership isn't enough. Croatia wants to see documentation from Arkansas affirming the idea. Given that no such documentation exists (or could ever exist) for any U.S. state (individual states can't put international treaties in place), while Croatia in theory should allow Americans to purchase property in Croatia (because Croatians can own in America), in reality, it balks. When we came to this bump in the road during the purchase process for our farmhouse in Istria, we had to reapply for title as Irish citizens. Fortunately for us, we hold both U.S. and Irish passports. If you don't hold a second passport, the workaround would be to purchase the property in the name of a Croatian corporation (noting that this could have negative tax implications).

16 Sometimes Really Cheap Isn't a Good Deal

A friend recently forwarded information to me about cheap lots on a Caribbean island. Prices started at $7,550. That's an attention-getter, right?

In fact, this sounds-too-good-to-be-true offer (like every such offer I've come across in nearly 30 years seeking out real estate investment opportunities overseas) is just that—too good to be true. Property this cheap generally falls short on some or all of the three points that matter in any property investment—location, size, and infrastructure.

In the case of the Caribbean lots I'm thinking of, upon closer inspection, I found that they were not, in fact, Caribbean lots. They were lots on an island in the Caribbean, true, but they were far from the sea. They also lacked infrastructure and were being sold without an access road and without electricity. The developer promised to build a way in, but once built (I'd suggest, *if* built), it would be up to the lot owners to maintain the access. The developer never intended to provide electricity to the lots. His plan was to put up poles. The electric company, he suggested, would have to come behind him to string the wire and flip the switch.

Finally, the lots were really small—about one-tenth of an acre, which is 418 square meters, or 4,500 square feet. The developer suggested that a buyer might want to invest in more than one if he intended to build a house.

Bottom line, I'm not sure you'd want one of these lots if someone offered to give it to you free, not once you'd factored in all the costs you would incur to hold and maintain the lot, and never mind the costs associated with actually trying to build on the lot and live in this "development," which was located well outside the town services area. You would have to provide your own water and wastewater systems.

To be fair, the developer addressed these issues openly on his website. In fact, he was more up-front than many foreign property developers I've had experience with over the years. Still, you've got to know how to interpret what you're being told. In this case, would-be owners were advised that their best option for potable water would be to catch rainwater and store it in a cistern. That can work, but again, you've got to add the associated costs to the price of the lot to be able to make a fair comparison to the price of a lot in a development where central water is being provided.

In addition, buyers of these lots had to install their own septic systems to deal with wastewater. Again, fair enough, but remember that each of these lots was only 4,500 square feet. That's not a lot of space to work with. And a septic system is another cost that needed to be added to the price of a lot to make a realistic comparison to the cost of a lot in a development providing central wastewater treatment.

How do you compare prices for lots in different developments where the services and amenities vary greatly? You essentially have to do your own appraisal. Start with the lot price, add in the costs of the extras you'll have to provide yourself (for example, water and wastewater treatment), and then divide the total cost by the number of square meters being purchased.

Let's look at another example, comparing two developments I know on the coast of Panama. One is a master-planned community with full infrastructure and amenities. The other is a basic lotification providing a central road and electricity. The lotification project is selling ocean-view lots at $30 a square meter. The average size is 3,000 square meters, meaning an average lot cost of $90,000. Although owners have access to aboveground electricity in this development, you have to make the connection to the nearest pole yourself. You also have to drill your own well or design a catchment system for drinking water, and you have to install your own septic system. If you want Internet, you'll have to provide that, too. In this case, that means a satellite system.

The total cost for these services would be about $15,000, meaning your $90,000 lot would, in fact, cost you about $105,000, that is, $35 per square meter, as opposed to the $30 advertised. That's almost 20 percent more than the list price. This is for a lot in a development with no amenities (no clubhouse, no central pool, no restaurant, etc.) and no direct access to the beach.

The master-planned community I'm thinking of on the same coast is selling lots for $44 a square meter. Included among the amenities are central water, central wastewater management, underground electricity to each lot, paved roads, and central Internet access. In addition, the plan calls for a clubhouse and a long list of other amenities. Plus, this property includes about a kilometer of beachfront, to which every lot owner has direct access.

On the other hand, amenities and services must be maintained. In the planned community, you'll have higher HOA fees than as an owner in the lotification, where the only thing to maintain are the dirt roads.

I indicated earlier that you might not want one of the "Caribbean" lots I was describing if someone offered it to you free. The associated hassles and carrying costs wouldn't be worth it to me, but you might have different priorities and objectives. A supercheap lot like this one could make sense for you, depending on your circumstances. My point is to be sure that you know what you're really buying and what it's really going to cost you, all told. When shopping and considering options, make sure that you're comparing apples to apples, one location to another, one property to another, as best you can.

17 Margarita Madness and How to Avoid It

You and your significant other are on a well-deserved vacation in the Caribbean, enjoying two sun-filled weeks staying in a resort hotel on the shores of Ambergris Caye, off the coast of Belize. A few days into your stay, while you're reading on the beach one afternoon, a well-tanned American gentleman approaches you.

"Hello," he says. "I've noticed you guys out here these past few days. Are you enjoying your stay? Sure is beautiful here, isn't it?"

"Yes!" you agree enthusiastically. How could you disagree? You haven't enjoyed yourself this much in, well, you can't remember the last time you enjoyed yourself this much.

"I've been living here full-time for three years," the guy continues. "I moved here from Texas. No intention of going back. I don't think I could ever leave this place. This is paradise."

Again, how could you disagree? So you don't.

"Have you been to the bar down the beach?" your new friend asks. "It's a great place to watch the sunset and to meet other Americans like me, living here full-time. I'm heading over there a little later. Maybe you'd like to come along? Margaritas are on me."

You go to meet your new friend at his favorite bar. He treats you to a couple of rounds of margaritas while sharing more of his story. He came on vacation just like you and fell in love. He then returned to Texas, wrapped up his affairs there, and came back down as quickly as he was able. Now he tries to help other Americans find their own piece of this paradise. He's opened a real estate agency—American Realty. If you're interested he could show you around a little in the morning. Take you on a tour of the island. There's so much to see, and it's all so beautiful.

By the end of the evening, you've agreed to meet the guy in the morning. Next morning, he shows up in a golf cart. How charming. He takes you up and down the coast of the little island, showing you one beautiful stretch of white sand after another.

"That little house there is for sale," he mentions, almost as an afterthought at one point. "And a little farther up the coast, a new development is breaking ground. That's really the place to buy right now, because you can get in for preconstruction prices. We could stop by and take a quick look if you'd like."

You stop. You look. The guy pulls out watercolor drawings of what the development will look like. The pool, the dock, the sunset from your balcony.

"No pressure," he says, "but you'd need to move quick to get in on that preconstruction deal. As soon as they finish such-and-such infrastructure, prices are going up."

You and your significant other return to your hotel room. You flip through the brochure the agent left with you. You have a couple of more margaritas while watching another of this island's glorious sunsets.

"Let's do it!" you agree. It's fate. Kismet. Meant to be.

You call the guy back the next day, sign a contract, and make a down payment—maybe with your American Express (handy that he takes credit cards).

I call it Margarita Madness, and it happens far more often than you might imagine. I've watched it play out dozens of times personally and have heard dozens of other Margarita Madness tales secondhand. I recommend you guard against it. Tequila and real estate don't mix.

Not all purchases made under these circumstances turn out to be mistakes, but many do. Not necessarily because the buyer decides he doesn't, in fact, want to own in that location. More often, the problem has to do with the particulars of the purchase. Buying that quick, while operating in vacation mode and under the influence of Caribbean moonlight and island margaritas, how can you be sure what you're buying? You can't, really. These kinds of purchases are a bad idea because they're made with a minimum (sometimes with an utter lack) of due diligence.

Remember the realities I've introduced to you here: the importance of verifying the history of ownership, for example, as well as the importance of vetting the developer, researching any restrictions on foreign ownership, understanding how best to take title, preparing for carrying costs and tax implications, and being clear in your exit strategy.

If you visit a place on vacation and like it, great. File that fact away. Return home and begin your research. Plan a second visit, this one more for due diligence and scouting than snorkeling and sunbathing. It may seem more convenient to act while you're already in the country (that's what the agent is counting on). In fact, it's just silly. How many times have you visited new a destination in the United States for a first time and, while there, bought a piece of real estate? You wouldn't act so hastily back home. You want to be more careful when making a real estate purchase overseas, not less. Don't let the sultry weather and the abundance of cheap alcohol conspire to cloud your clarity on that point.

IV

How to Buy Real Estate Overseas

Eight Easy Steps

When Lief and I arrived in Waterford years ago and decided we wanted to own a home of our own there, we set out to find one the way that any Americans would set out to buy a house. We dropped by a real estate agent's office in the center of Waterford City. We sat down with Mr. O'Shea and gave him the rundown on the kind of house we were looking for: Georgian, stone, at least three bedrooms and three baths, with a bit of land for a garden, maybe an old barn for a pony. Mr. O'Shea seemed to take our criteria under advisement and suggested a time later in the week when one of his agents could show us available properties. That first day out, we saw four houses, not one of which in any way fit the description we'd given to Mr. O'Shea in his office. Instead, his agent kept taking us to see new-built "bungalows" in "estates," as the Irish refer to the suburban housing subdivisions that were popping up all across the country when we arrived on the scene. I refused to get out of the car to walk through the fourth place. It looked just like the three we'd already seen and that I'd already explained weren't anything like what we were interested in buying.

The Celtic Tiger was an established economic phenomenon by the time we took up residence in Waterford, and the better part of the money that boom was throwing off was being plowed into real estate—building it, buying it, selling it, one Irishman to another. Dozens of the housing estates of the kind Mr. O'Shea's team was so intent on introducing to us were being developed across the Emerald Isle in the start of what proved to be one of the biggest Ponzi schemes in history. Over the next seven years that we lived in Ireland, the real estate market in this country continued up and up and up. It was a self-fueling spiral, as farmers sold at big prices to developers who then put their money in the banks for the banks to lend to the developers' buyers.

This chaotically expanding Irish marketplace of the late 1990s was our introduction to shopping for real estate in a foreign country. It took us months to begin to realize how much we didn't know of what we didn't know. I'd like to save you the frustration and the confusion that we suffered as we felt our way through that first purchase in Ireland and other early property buys. Here, therefore, is how you buy real estate overseas, in eight easy steps.

18

Get on a Plane

Buying a piece of real estate overseas isn't like buying a stock. You shouldn't do it over the Internet.

I've bought and sold property in 21 countries, from developer lots to beachfront parcels to develop myself, from rental apartments to entire buildings for rehab, from preconstruction condos to old and in need of complete renovation. Some of these investments have been home runs, most have made money, a few have fizzled, and one imploded. One common denominator of those investments I've made that have proven disappointing or downright disastrous is that I didn't get on a plane to go see them in person myself before buying.

My worst foreign property purchase was made on the recommendation of an employee at the time. A former marketing manager played golf with a friend who knew a guy who had connections with a preconstruction opportunity in what he reported to be a superhot, up-and-coming market. This was a decade ago, during the golden age of global property investing, when everyone believed that values could only continue to go up. I'd been to the country where this hot-tip investment was located but never to the town in question. I researched online, followed up with the developer, and persuaded myself that it didn't matter that I didn't know the location and hadn't visited the site personally. My marketing manager's friend's guy had.

Today I'm embarrassed to admit this investment. What was I thinking? The truth is that I wasn't thinking. I allowed my judgment to be clouded by projection spreadsheets.

A few months after signing the contract and sending the down payment, I finally had time to get on a plane and visit the property. I knew within 5 minutes that I'd made a mistake. The town was unappealing, nowhere I would ever want to spend time, and the building I'd bought into was common and nondescript. Further, it was but one of a number of similar buildings also under construction at the same time in the same area. Too much nonspecial inventory coming online into a market I perceived as too depressed to absorb it all.

To make a long story short, the building was completed, and I had to close on the deal. The market was as depressed as it appeared. I was reduced to competing with all my fellow speculator landlords for renters. Not enough of them to go around meant low occupancy rates and low rents.

Every investor needs at least one big loser experience. This was mine. It taught me what I now consider one of the most important lessons I've learned related to buying real estate overseas: Don't buy sight unseen, and don't take anyone else's word for what you're buying into. Get on a plane and go see for yourself.

19 Figure Your Budget

Start any overseas property experience with a budget, remembering that the sales price you agree to for whatever you eventually decide to buy is only the start of it. To this amount, remember to add transaction costs (see Appendix A). The biggest cost of acquisition of a piece of property overseas is what's typically called a transfer fee (or tax) or stamp duty. This is a straightforward tax on real estate transactions, and most countries charge one. In Europe, transfer fees can be as much as 12.5 percent (Belgium) or as little as 0 percent (several countries), depending on the purchase price of the property. In places like Ireland and Croatia, where no property taxes are imposed (this is in the process of changing in Ireland, where a property tax is expected to come into effect in 2014), you can view the transfer tax as prepaying the property tax if that makes it easier to bear. No matter how you look at it, it's something to take seriously. In parts of the world that charge double-digit transfer taxes, flipping real estate can be expensive, too expensive to make sense as an investment strategy and so expensive that a would-be retiree- or lifestyle-buyer doesn't want to buy wrong. Reselling and buying again will eat into your nest egg.

A true transfer tax isn't recoverable. However, some countries, including Nicaragua, for example, charge the seller a tax at the time of closing that is sometimes referred to as a transfer tax but that is really a capital gains withholding tax. Note that although this fee is charged of the seller, the seller typically passes it on to the buyer. When charged, this fee is a way for the country to make sure it gets paid at least some of the income tax due on the capital gains from the eventual resale of a piece of property. Governments of countries with active foreign property markets understand that most foreign buyers aren't going to file tax returns when selling a real estate holding in that country. The tax charged at the point of sale is meant to bring any eventual tax owed on any eventual capital gain forward. If by some chance the withholding tax is more than what the capital gains tax would be (usually it won't be), you can then file a tax return to try to get a refund of the difference.

Other expenses to remember in your acquisition budget include attorney, notary, and registration fees. In most cases these costs are nominal, but again, you want to make sure you know what they are before you start shopping so that you can factor them into your overall capital requirements. Belgium, again, is at the high end for these transaction costs; notary costs in this country can run as high as 4 percent of the purchase price.

Note that unlike a notary in the United States, a notary in a civil law country is a licensed attorney with an additional license (specific for performing the duties of a notary) or title granted by the government. These are semigovernmental agents who act as gatekeepers for official documents, including property titles. In France, for example, your *notaire* manages the entire real estate purchase process (meaning you don't need a regular attorney; your *notaire* takes the place of an attorney), including the title check and the transfer of title. In other countries, the notary is simply the official registration agent.

Attorney and notary costs should run 0.5 to 1 percent of the transaction cost, with the percentage decreasing as the value of the transaction increases. Unfortunately, in some Latin American countries, some attorneys notice how much real estate agents make from property transactions and get the idea that they should make more. The result is that attorney fees in this part of the world can be all over the board. Confirm the fee for a particular transaction with your attorney before you begin to process any paperwork with him or her. Don't assume that these rates will be comparable to rates quoted you by another attorney.

Registration fees should amount to less than 0.5 percent of the purchase price but are typically charged as a set fee, rather than as a percentage of the purchase price.

The final cost to remember when figuring your capital requirement budget for the purchase of real estate in another country is the real estate agent's fee. In many countries, the seller pays this; however, in some markets, this cost is shared, and you as the buyer will be expected to pay part (perhaps half). Argentina, Croatia, and Italy are three examples where this is the case. The reality is that, as the buyer, you're really always paying all the real estate agent's fee. It's just that in most places it's included in the list price, rather than charged as a separate and additional cost.

There are always anomalies. In France, the agent's fee is included in the list price by some agencies and not included by others. In this country, agencies should note on their listing sheets whether the fee is included in the list price. If you don't see this detailed on a listing sheet you're reviewing, ask for clarification. Note that this difference (whether the fee is included in the list price or not) should be by agency, not by agent working for that agency and not by property among the same agency's listings.

One good example of how the associated costs of acquisition can accumulate to become a significant part of the total acquisition budget is Belize. In this country, the standard stamp duty for the purchase of real estate is 5 percent. You get an exemption on the first $10,000 of the purchase price (saving you $500). In addition, though, if you're buying a piece of property from a developer, you must also pay a 12.5 percent sales tax. (Note that this additional fee does not apply to resale purchases.) Most developers don't include this tax in their list prices, but some do. You should ask the developer at the start of the negotiating process so that you know exactly what you'll be liable for at closing. These two fees alone amount to 17.5 percent. In addition, you'll have your attorney's fees.

I detail the round-trip costs for 20 key markets in Appendix A. Understand, though, that governments can change fee structures at any time and do. During the seven years we lived in Ireland, the government changed the stamp duty structure at least five times. It was their attempt to cool the speculation going on in that country's real estate market at that time. At one point (fortunately not when we purchased), the top rate of Irish stamp duty was 9 percent!

The bulk of your budget is the purchase price in a cash-only market or the down payment in places where foreigners can borrow or negotiate seller terms. You know how much capital you have available for any purchase. Make your total budget known to every property agent you work with. Don't waste your time or the agent's by looking at property that costs more than you want or are able to spend.

20 Build an In-Country Network of Reliable Contacts

When shopping in the United States, you entertain any conversation about the purchase of a piece of real estate taking many things for granted, as we've been discussing. You're confident not only that you don't have to worry about things like history of ownership and promised future amenities, but also that in the event something goes wrong, you'll have some recourse. You assume that you could file your grievance with some oversight agency. Worst case, there'll always be somebody you could sue, right?

There's no Honduran government agency that regulates the sale of real estate to foreign buyers, and how are you going to sue somebody in Nicaragua? You aren't. So you need to make sure you don't end up in a situation where that seems to be your only option. How do you do that? You engage a good attorney to protect your interests.

Your attorney is your most important ally when buying, selling, or renting real estate in any overseas market. Although you might buy real estate in the United States without ever thinking of engaging an attorney, I suggest that you never buy real estate in another country without first thing, before you do anything else, finding a local attorney you can trust who speaks real English, who has experience working with foreigners, and who, critically, works for you. Your attorney should not work for the seller or the property developer, but for you and sharing doesn't count. If you're sharing an attorney with the developer or seller, whose interests come first in his mind when an issue arises? Note that this is what most developers in most developing markets push for. "My attorney's great," the developer you're intending to buy from will tell you. "He has helped dozens of Americans buy here. He knows his stuff. You'll love him. I'll put you in touch."

Resist the temptation. It will seem the easy, efficient solution, but it puts you at a disadvantage throughout the entire purchase process.

That's the first important point to understand about engaging an attorney to represent your interests as you shop for real estate in any foreign market. The second has to do with language. What do I mean when I say you need an attorney who speaks real English? I mean that you need to find an attorney who understands what you say when you speak to him not only literally but figuratively, as well. Think of the differences between U.S. English, British English, and Aussie English and the misunderstandings that can occur as a result. Now imagine you're speaking to someone who learned his English with the help of a tutor later in life or someone who learned to speak English by watching MTV as a kid (I've known many people in many places around the world for whom this has been the case). That person may understand the words you're speaking, but that doesn't mean he's following your underlying meanings, your slang, your metaphors, your points of reference, and so on. When your money is on the table, you want someone who processes the nuances of your instructions as well as the literal details.

Finding a good local attorney who speaks English and has had experience with foreign property buyers should be your number one priority when you enter a new market with the intent to buy. Your first order of business is best accomplished before you begin scouting, searching, or viewing. How do you find a good attorney in a foreign country? By referral. You don't want to make this decision based on an Internet search. You want to work with an attorney found via some personal recommendation, ideally the personal recommendation of a fellow expat. Ask everyone you communicate with in any market where you're thinking about buying for an attorney reference. Identify two or three attorneys whose names come up again and again. Contact them. Interview them, by e-mail and then by phone. Take time to get to know them.

Once you've made this all-important first connection, you can build out your in-country network of contacts from there. The attorney you choose to work with can recommend real estate agents, bankers, accountants, even carpenters, contractors, electricians, and—very important—other expats who've already invested in the country. This is how I've built networks of contacts that I trust and that in some cases I've now worked with for going on three decades in dozens of countries.

In addition, when trying to get your head around a new market, seek out and spend time with locals not in the real estate business, from taxi drivers to waitresses, and shop owners to bartenders. Their insights into the real estate market can be most valuable. In Medellín, for example, on one of my first scouting trips, I had one of my most helpful conversations with an antiques dealer whose shop I stopped in one Saturday afternoon. Smart, successful local businesspeople can give you valuable insights into a market that a real estate agent might neglect to mention.

Ask everyone you speak with the same questions. You'll be surprised by the variety of answers you'll get. Some will be completely contradictory. In some cases, you might ask six people the same question and get six different responses. Our first scouting trip in Medellín, we asked one real estate agent we met with if it were possible for a foreigner to open a bank account in Colombia. "Yes, of course, no problem. You just need your passport," he told us. We asked another real estate agent we met with the same question. "To open a bank account in Colombia, a foreigner needs a *cedula*. Do you know what that is?" he asked. Yes, we knew what that was—a residency card issued only to those with legal foreign residence status. That left us out.

Here's a checklist of questions you should also ask everyone you encounter in any new market you enter:

- Which are considered the nicest neighborhoods?
- Which are considered the up-and-coming neighborhoods?
- How much does an apartment or a house cost? Boil this down to a per-square-meter price so that you can compare among areas within the country and among other countries.
- Where are most foreigners buying? Why?
- What types of properties are most foreigners buying (one-bedroom apartments, houses, undeveloped land, etc.)? Why?
- Are most foreigners buying for personal use or for investment?
- Is there an active rentals market? Short term, long term, or both?
- How much would a particular property rent for per month long term or per week short term?
- Where would you (speaking to a real estate agent, an attorney, a business owner, an expat, or a taxi driver) invest right now? Why?
- In which direction is the market moving?

Ask general questions about the local economy and local industry. Ask about the current president or whoever is in charge of running things. Not to be political but to get a read on the political situation from the man on the street. Ask about taxes. Are they high? Do people pay them? How are they collected? Is there a property tax? On what value is it based? Again, you'll be amazed at the variety of answers you'll receive. All this input, conflicting as it will seem, will help give you the lay of the land. The more conflicting the responses, the wilder the market.

The next step is to begin to get a handle on procedures. For this, you'll need help from your attorney. Here's a checklist of questions to ask him or her:

- What are the transaction costs for buying and selling real estate? You'll want to know the "round-trip" costs, as I refer to them, for a single piece of property. In some markets, it is more expensive to buy than to sell and vice versa. You don't want to find out too late that, while it cost only 2 percent to get into an investment, it's going to cost you 15 percent to get out.

- What is the buying process? What documents are required? What is a typical down payment? Are there any local nuances you should know? In many emerging markets, for example, you'll be told that it's common practice for the purchase price for a piece of real estate to be understated (perhaps significantly) on the sales documents. This can have advantages (when it comes to paying property taxes, for example), but it also can create problems down the road, vis-à-vis capital gains tax and foreign exchange controls if they exist. Even if you're assured that "everyone does it," I recommend that you don't. Even if it means paying the seller a little more (as it can), insist that the full purchase price be represented on the purchase documents.

Exchange controls are an important point to understand with the help of your attorney. Will you have any trouble taking your money back out of the country when you decide you're ready to do so?

While you're playing private detective and asking everyone you meet the same series of questions, you also want to be observing. As you learn your way around the area, do you notice signs of an active economy? Are people out at the malls and restaurants shopping, spending? What's the infrastructure like? Are the roads well maintained? Are the parks and public areas taken care of? Do you see garbage in the streets or on the sidewalks?

A strong local economy can translate into one possible exit strategy for your real estate purchase. If no local economy exists or if the local economy is small and limited, then you're likely going to be limited to selling on to another foreigner when the time comes for you to cash out. This is the case in many resort markets in Mexico and Spain, for example. Having a local market can reduce your investment risk.

During your first visit to any new market, see as many properties in as many different neighborhoods and areas as you have time for. You want to get a feel for the type of construction, the options for building materials, common amenities, and so forth. See how apartments are typically laid out. Is space well used? Collect and catalogue every listing sheet for every property you view. Then go home. Don't buy anything your first trip no matter how tempted you are. Take all your boots-on-the-ground information with you back wherever you came from. Sift through it. Compare responses. Check facts with as many sources as possible.

An in-country network of reliable contacts is the first part of the prepurchase infrastructure you need to create. The second part has to do with logistics. Here's a checklist for the administrative infrastructure you're going to need in any country where you purchase real estate:

- A local bank account or whatever alternative is going to allow you to transfer money into the country and then pay local expenses. In Colombia, for example, you'll have trouble opening a bank account as a nonresident foreigner. It'll be much easier (and just as effective) to open what's called a fiduciary account. This is the equivalent of a Schwab account in the United States.
- The ability to wire funds from your home base bank account using fax or phone instructions. This may mean switching banks at home, as some U.S. banks require you to come to your bank branch in person to organize a wire transfer. This won't work if you happen to be in Belize, say, or Italy at the time you decide you need to send the wire.
- The holding structure for the property if you aren't going to take title in your own name—a real estate holding company or an LLC, for example (more on this in Chapter 24).
- A bank account for that company. I recommend you start the process to open this account as soon as the company is set up, even if you don't intend to use it for some time. It's increasingly difficult to open a bank

account anywhere in the world as a nonresident, and it's more difficult still to open a nonresident corporate account.

Once an in-country network of support is established and the necessary purchase infrastructure in place, you're ready for the next step—finding the piece of property you want to buy.

21 Identify a Purchase

U nless you're buying strictly for personal use and know without question where you want to purchase, the biggest challenge of buying property overseas can be identifying where to buy. I've offered recommendations, depending on your objectives and interests. However, my recommendations are big picture. Spain and Ireland offer crisis-investing opportunities, Panama and Colombia are markets of abundant opportunity, and so on. Deciding that you'd like to own in Panama because you like the idea of buying into a bull market with a long run still ahead of it is a great starting point, but it's only a starting point. Do you want to buy in Panama City or the mountains? On the Pacific coast outside Panama City or in Bocas del Toro in the Caribbean? On the Azuero Peninsula or one of the islands in the Bay of Panama? Unimproved land or a rental apartment? Preconstruction or commercial? I could offer positive arguments and make specific suggestions in each case, but you'd still face many decisions. How do you move from the very general notion that you'd like to own real estate in a particular country to identifying the specific piece of property you want to buy?

It takes time and what I refer to as "being in the market." When you target a country or a region as a place where you think you want to buy, you need then to work to position yourself so that you're ready to act when the right opportunity presents itself. You do this by researching, scouting, and staying connected. This is where the in-country network of support you've built, starting with a local attorney you trust, begins to pay off. When you've identified a big-picture location for purchase, make everyone you know in that location aware that you're in the market, looking for an opportunity. Give them an idea of what kind of property you're shopping for (size, specific location, intended use) and your budget.

You can't wake up one morning and decide you're going to invest in a rental property in Panama, a Pacific coast beach house in Nicaragua, or an apartment in Paris. Well, you could, I guess, and you could then proceed quickly to buy. But, operating in that context, the chances that you'll get the best deal possible are slim and the chances that things won't play out the way you hope are not.

You need to be in a market long enough to understand the difference between the local market and the gringo one. You need the experience of vetting opportunities and of communicating with sellers. You need to determine your own idea of comparables and of what a piece of property of the description you're looking to buy should cost. You aren't going to accomplish those things in a single visit to a country or after a few weeks of Internet research. To buy right, you need to give the in-country contacts and resources you've developed a chance to connect with you in real time. You need to leverage their boots on the ground, because, unless you're taking up temporary residence in the place yourself while conducting your property search (not a bad idea but usually not possible), you don't have boots on the ground of your own.

My most recent property purchase was an apartment in Medellín, Colombia. Colombia was a new market for me when I decided I wanted to invest there. Even though I'd bought real estate in many other foreign countries many times before, I moved slowly. I solicited a local attorney recommendation from an expat friend who had recently bought in Medellín himself. I traveled to Medellín to meet the attorney in person, and then, with his help, I developed a network of connections, including three real estate agents (one gringo, two local), a banker, and a contractor (as I knew I was shopping for a renovation project). I returned to the country five times over 10 months, each time expanding my network and furthering my education. Finally, after nearly a year of focused effort and after viewing dozens of apartments for sale, I made a choice and an offer. A year is maybe excessive. I've purchased in other new markets after six months of attention or less. My point is that, even if you've got years of experience at this, it takes time to identify a purchase, especially if you're targeting what for you is a new market.

22 Negotiate the Purchase

The actual real estate purchase process varies by country, but, generally speaking, there are three steps:

1. Make an offer.
2. Sign a sale agreement.
3. Sign a sales contract.

To you and me it may seem that the sale agreement and the sales contract should be the same thing, but, in most countries, they aren't. In most of the world, the first one is not a purchase agreement but a "promise" to sell; the second one is the closing document that results in the property being titled in the new owner's name. Specifically, here's how this typically works:

1. **You make an offer.** Most offers are made in person or by telephone, either directly from the buyer to the seller or through a real estate agent. Offers are not typically conveyed in writing. Depending on the market, your offer can be a starting point for a price negotiation. You should seek some advice in advance from others with experience in the market as to what's culturally acceptable on this front. Should you make a low-ball offer with the intention of meeting the seller midway between that number and the asking price? Should you offer 10 percent less than is being asked? Should you expect a counteroffer? If the

seller accepts your offer, are you bound to follow through, if not by law perhaps by local custom? And so on.

2. **You execute a sales agreement (*promesa de compraventa* in Spanish or *compromise de vente* in French).** This can be an optional step depending on the country and whether you're ready to move to the closing right away. The *promesa* is a binding contract that outlines the terms of the sale to come. It's similar in function to a real estate sales contract in the United States and includes details for the down payment (including under what conditions it is refundable), spells out terms for full payment, sets a closing date, and specifies penalties for default. If you're buying in a country where it's possible and where you're planning to obtain local bank financing for the purchase (in many European countries, for example), your sales agreement should also contain a condition stating that, if your application for a mortgage is not successful, your deposit will be refunded.

Note that, in France, you have a seven-day cooling off period from the date you sign the *compromise de vente,* during which time you can withdraw from the sale without penalty but the seller cannot. A word of caution: I know a couple who bought a home and then decided during the cooling-off period that they had made a mistake. They tried to contact the *notaire* and then the agent on the seventh day only to find that it was a national holiday in France and both the attorney's and the agent's offices were closed. The sale went through. Moral of the story: Make sure your *notaire* will be available during your cooling-off period.

3. **You complete the closing documents (*escritura de compraventa* in Spanish *or acte de vente* in French).** The *escritura* (or *acte de vente,* etc.) is the final document and serves as the deed to the property once it's been recorded in the local property registry. Until this document is registered, the title is still in the name of previous owner. Your notary generally should record the new *escritura* the day you sign it, but sometimes, depending on the country, this document might not be recorded until a few days later.

In some extreme cases (Croatia is an example), it can be that the sales agreement is recorded (blocking any other sale of the property by the previous owner) while the government processes their paperwork to approve you as a foreign buyer. When we bought our farmhouse in Croatia, the actual title wasn't registered until more than a year after we'd paid for the property. In the meantime, again, the executed sales agreement was recorded to protect us against the previous owner selling the place that we'd already bought.

Your attorney or *notaire* will manage the purchase process for you, but you need to understand at least the big picture of what's going on and what you should expect to be happening each step along the way. If you don't speak the local language, your attorney should provide a translation of all the documents you'll need to sign. Note, however, that everywhere in the world, a contract must be signed and registered in the local language to be legally valid.

The timing of each step becomes important if you're not living in the country. You don't want to book a flight to wherever you're buying for the closing of your purchase only to have the closing delayed. If you don't plan to return to the country for the closing, then you should obtain a power of attorney in that country before you leave, as it is always easier to do this locally than long distance. Depending on the country, you may need to have the power of attorney notarized (by the embassy of the country where you're buying) or apostilled. Obtaining an apostille requires a trip to your state's Secretary of State's office (or other similar national government office if you're not in the United States).

A typical down payment in most of the world is 10 percent, but depending on what you're buying where, you may have to put down as much as 40 percent. In the case of the apartment I recently purchased in Medellín, for example, the seller wanted 30 percent down because we were foreign buyers. We understood his concerns and agreed.

The down payment is typically made at the time you sign the sale agreement.

The period between the signing of the *promesa* and the signing of the *escritura* (that is, between the sale agreement and the closing) is your chance to carry out your final due diligence. You'll want to have vetted the purchase in advance of signing the sale agreement, first, because this is a binding document and, second, because the length of time and/or the limits on the conditions you can include in the sale agreement typically do not allow for complete due diligence.

Some countries (Panama, for example) have computerized central property registries making it easy for any attorney to check on the history of ownership for any property in the country. All that's needed is the property's registry number. Other places, where there is no such centralized property registry (Nicaragua), your attorney will have to go to the local mayor's office to check the title registry locally and in person.

This is a general overview of the property purchase process anywhere in the world. More specifically, this is how it works in most of Europe and in most of Latin America. However, if and when you eventually decide to purchase a home in another country, ask your real estate attorney for a complete outline of the local purchase process. He should have this in writing in English. If he doesn't, you should think about finding another attorney (one who is more experienced working with foreign buyers).

23 Close the Deal

Around the enormous table sat five adult siblings, three with spouses, two with attorneys, one with a grown son, plus the real estate agent for the seller, his two representatives, our real estate agent, our agent's boss, and my husband and me. It was the summer of 2003 in Buenos Aires. Over the preceding 12 months, Lief and I had bought three apartments in this city in the wake of Argentina's 2001 currency debacle and subsequent property crash. We arranged our schedules to be able to participate in the closing of the third apartment personally. We were purchasing from the five children of the elderly owner who had recently died in the apartment in question.

Argentines traditionally (with good reason) don't trust banks. Following the 2001 collapse, they really didn't trust banks. Real estate closings, therefore, were all-cash transactions that take place in the offices of currency houses, like the one where Lief and I sat that sunny summer morning. Papers went back and forth among siblings and attorneys, attorneys and agents, attorneys and attorneys. Then the agent for the currency house appeared. She had the cash. Lief and I had wired down our funds a couple of days beforehand so that the required cash bundles could be prepared. It was a $220,000 transaction.

The cash wasn't simply going from buyer (us) to seller. There were multiple sellers, each due a different percentage of the purchase amount. Thus, the bill counter, the kind of machine drug dealers and casinos might employ, was moved into the room. Sister A got $22,000. Sister B got $35,000. Big brother who had been living in the house with his mother until she died got more than $100,000. The agent in charge passed him a plastic-wrapped brick of $100 bills and some "change" in the form of smaller individual packages.

Each sibling had his or her own ideas about how best to transport his or her cash. Sister A stuffed much of it inside her bra. One brother had a money belt for his relatively small take. The other sister gave some to her husband, put some in her purse, and gave some to her son. The brother who got the brick of 100s had little option but to use a small duffle bag.

The real estate agents took their commissions, and the attorneys took their fees and the amount required to register the title, again, all in cash. After everyone had claimed what was due him, a small pile remained in the middle of the table, a few thousand dollars left over that belonged to the buyers (us). Lief walked out with around $3,000 in cash in his jacket pocket. He told me later that he wondered if some local gang had figured out when real estate closings were being transacted at these currency houses so they could post someone at the entrances of the buildings and mug people as they walked out on to the street. (None of us was robbed.) The entire transaction took about an hour, with most of the time spent counting out bills.

Most closings aren't this dramatic, although it's not uncommon for *campesinos* in Central America (country folk in this part of the world) to request all cash at closing. One guy I purchased land from in Panama years ago supposedly transported his money back to his shack of a house in the middle of nowhere in a black garbage bag. He didn't have a bank account (and probably didn't trust banks anyway).

The particulars of closing on a real estate transaction vary by country, but more typical than all cash is a cashier's check and a few signatures in front of a notary. Typically, you can avoid the entire process if you'd prefer by assigning your attorney a power of attorney, allowing her to sign the closing documents and manage the closing on your behalf. I'd suggest, though, being on hand in person at least for your first one or two closings and certainly if you buy in Argentina, just for the experience.

Even if you intend to be on hand yourself for a closing, I recommend that you process the paperwork to assign your attorney your power of attorney in advance anyway. Things happen. If for some reason at the last minute you're unable to make the trip to sign the closing documents yourself, having the power of attorney in place as a backup could save you from not being able to register the title in your name because of missing signatures or even losing the purchase (and your deposit) altogether.

If you're getting a mortgage for the purchase, you may need to give your attorney a separate power of attorney allowing him to sign the mortgage documents (though sometimes you can sign these in advance of the official closing). Confirm with your bank what you need to have in place to ensure that this part of the closing goes smoothly.

Key, of course, to any property closing is the payment. Some of it could be via a mortgage, but for any purchase, at least part of the payment will be in cash, requiring you to get cash where it needs to be when it needs to be there. I discuss the challenges and considerations associated with accomplishing this in detail in Part V.

24 Take Title

I f you purchase a piece of real estate in another country, should you have the ownership documents issued in your name or perhaps in the name of a corporation? If a corporation, should it be a local company (formed in the jurisdiction where you're purchasing) or one based somewhere else?

To make the right choice for how to hold the title for a piece of foreign property you that intend to purchase, you should consider two things: taxes and your estate.

Understand the tax obligations both in the country where you're buying and also in the United States if you're an American. Likewise, implications for your estate should be considered both locally and back home.

Let's take Panama as an example. The typical way to hold real estate in this country is through a Panamanian corporation. This provides a positive tax effect in Panama whenever you resell, because you're not, in fact, selling the piece of property but the company that owns it. This minimizes the capital gains tax. On the other hand, owning a piece of property in a Panamanian corporation can create a negative U.S. tax effect for an American. Specifically, this can result in the gains being taxed at income rather than capital gains rates. You have to weigh the potential liabilities.

Regarding the estate issue, you need to make sure you understand both inheritance laws and estate taxes in the country where you're buying. Let's take France as an example. The inheritance laws in this country may surprise you and certainly can result in your property ending up somewhere other than where you'd like it to go following your death unless you have a will that the French will recognize. Particular issues arise if you are in a second marriage, for example, or have stepchildren to whom you'd like to leave some ownership of a French asset. If you die without a will that is valid in France, this is not what will happen. The default French inheritance distribution follows blood. Without proper planning, your assets could end up going to your uncle (or some other random relative) rather than to the people you'd like to have them. However, you can avoid French probate altogether if you hold your French real estate asset not in your name but in the name of an SCI, which is a French company formed specifically for the purpose of holding property.

You see, therefore, the importance of thinking through ownership structures before making any investment in foreign real estate. Specifically, what are your options?

The first would be to hold the piece of property in your own name. This is the most simple and straightforward strategy and can make sense if you plan to hold the property for only a short period of time. However, generally speaking, this is probably not the best way to hold property in any country. First, it's typically not the best option in the context of the local inheritance laws (as I explained in my France example). In addition, though, you want to remember probate. If you hold a piece of property in another country in your name, your heirs will have to go through probate in that country. If you hold property in your name in three other countries, your heirs will have to go through probate in all three. Having to go through probate in a foreign country to claim assets you've left them could change the way your heirs remember you. (You'll be dead, of course, so maybe you don't care.)

That said, there are cases when holding property in your personal name has benefits that override the probate concern. For example, in Argentina and Croatia, if you hold real estate in your personal name (as opposed to in that of a corporation), then you are not liable for capital gains tax when you resell.

The next option for holding real estate is an entity formed within the country where the property is located. As I mentioned, most buyers in Panama (including Panamanians) take title to their real estate in the name of a Panamanian corporation. This saves you the 2 percent real estate transfer tax when you resell the property (as long as you hold each property in a separate corporation) and can help to minimize capital gains taxes. Capital gains in Panama are currently taxed at 10 percent. However, when you sell your shares of the corporation that owns the real estate, you incur only a

5 percent withholding on the gross transaction value. Assuming your property has more than doubled in value since you bought it, you can simply opt not to file a tax return on the resale transaction, thereby effectively paying less than 10 percent on the gain. If the property value hasn't more than doubled, then you file a tax return to request a refund for the difference between the withholding and the actual tax due.

Note that shares of a corporation in a given country, although not real estate, are still an asset in that country, meaning there still can be a probate risk. The way to avoid that would be to create a parent company or trust to own the local corporation. That parent company or trust could be in your home country; however, it's probably better from the point of view of asset protection and privacy to use a third jurisdiction for this.

On the other hand, this can be more structuring than you want or need and layering structures like this can get complicated. Don't attempt it on your own. Seek legal advice both in the country where the property is located and in your home country, especially if you're an American.

The final option for how to hold a piece of property you buy in a foreign country is through a third country entity. For example, you could take title to your beach house in Nicaragua using a Belizean IBC. Again, though, this can be a more complicated structure than you want or need. In addition, many countries will require you to register the foreign entity locally for tax purposes. This can be difficult in situations where the country doesn't recognize the type of entity. I struggled with my recent purchase in Medellín, Colombia, for example, where I wanted to take title in the name of an LLC. This proved an uncommon approach in this jurisdiction.

In addition, setting up these kinds of entities comes at a cost. The setup for a Panamanian corporation costs about $1,000 (depending on the attorney). A Nevis LLC costs about $850. Then there are the annual carrying costs, which amount to about $500 for most foreign entities. These costs have to be weighed against the benefits of asset protection, avoiding probate, and minimizing the need for a will in the countries where you want to purchase.

If you are buying only a single piece of real estate in a single country, then the holding structure can and should be simple, maybe just one local entity. The important thing is to understand the tax and estate implications in the country where you're planning to buy and in your home country as well before you make a purchase. Changing directions midstream can be expensive. You don't want, for example, to have to retitle a piece of real estate in a foreign country (from your own name to that of a corporation, say). In most cases, this would mean paying the transfer tax again (even if you're transferring the asset from your individual name to that of an entity you own 100 percent), and the transfer tax can range from 1 to 12 percent of the property value at the time of the transfer. You want to get the titling right from the start.

25 Manage the Asset

Property ownership overseas can trigger particular tax liabilities. I've discussed taxes that can be associated with purchasing real estate in a foreign country. However, once you've made the investment, you can also have ongoing associated tax burdens. I'll address the generic ones first (that is, the ones that apply to everyone). Then I'll walk you through the specific U.S. tax implications you'll face as an American buying property overseas.

The most obvious ongoing tax associated with owning a piece of property anywhere is property tax. The good news is that not all countries impose one. If your frame of reference is a U.S. state where the property taxes are high, this can be another nice benefit of diversifying overseas in this way.

Property taxes in many countries are managed at the local level—by the municipality, as it were, which oversees collections and sometimes sets the rates. This means that, depending on the country, you may need to know where, exactly, you'll be buying before you can know what your property tax rates might be. Generally speaking, though, property taxes are lower most everywhere in the world than the U.S. average, and, again, not all countries charge them.

Sometimes, a country will exempt certain kinds of properties or certain kinds of purchases from property tax for certain periods of time, to encourage investment. This was the case in Panama over the past two decades or so, when the government offered a 20-year tax exemption to all new property purchases. (This exemption has since expired.) A property tax exemption or no property tax at all is great, of course, but property tax shouldn't be a determining factor for where you decide to invest and certainly not for where you choose to retire. In most of the world, it's a negligible expense.

Another tax related to owning real estate that you can encounter in some countries is what's referred to as a wealth tax. This is a tax on an individual's net worth. A wealth tax can be complicated to understand. If you surpass a threshold amount for total value of assets held in a country that imposes a wealth tax, you can be liable for the tax whether you're a resident or not. As a resident in a country that imposes a wealth tax, you'll likely be liable for the tax on your worldwide assets. Argentina, Colombia, Uruguay, and France all impose wealth taxes. You aren't liable for the tax on your worldwide assets in France or Colombia until you've been resident for five years, and, bottom line, given the available exemptions in most countries that impose a wealth tax, you aren't likely to be liable for much actual tax unless your net worth is significant.

A third tax to consider when investing in a piece of property in another country comes into play only if you rent out the place. In many jurisdictions, rental income is treated like ordinary income. Typically, you'll have to file a tax return in the country at the end of the year to report the rental income and to show the tax owed. Some countries, though, have figured out that foreign property owners don't always report rental revenues. This has led some countries to impose taxes at the source. Practically speaking, this means that in some places, your property/rental manager will be instructed to hold a percentage of the rental income you earn and hand it over to the government's tax authority. These withholding rates are typically onerous, with the intent of motivating you to file a full and proper income tax return at the end of the year (hopefully to claim back some of the withholding as a refund).

Some governments have gone so far as to make a proactive presumption that any nonprimary residence is a rental. They then charge you tax on a presumed rental value/income for your property. Spain does this. With so many foreign property owners who use their condos and villas only part-time and rent them out otherwise, the government wants to be sure it's getting a piece of all the rental income being generated within its jurisdiction. The flaw in this approach is obvious. Not every nonprimary residence is a rental and certainly not every nonprimary residence is rented out full-time. If you have a holiday home on the Spanish *costa* that you allow to sit empty when you aren't using it, you will not like this Spanish government tax policy.

Most countries allow you to deduct direct and related expenses against your rental income, including mortgage interest, management expenses, utilities if you're paying them (this would be the case for short-term rentals, for example), and any other direct expenses. What most countries don't allow you to deduct is depreciation. This is a U.S. accounting phenomenon that is also allowed for U.S. tax calculations but typically not elsewhere.

If you are a U.S. citizen holding a rental property in another country, it's treated more or less the same as a U.S. rental property for U.S. tax purposes. You are allowed the same expense deductions, including depreciation and the cost of travel to visit and check on the property. You report the rental income on a Schedule E, as you would for any U.S. rental income.

The complications for an American can arise from the tax liability in the country where the property is located. Without depreciation as an expense, you may have a profit in the foreign country and a loss on your U.S. taxes. The tax you pay in the foreign country can be used as a tax credit against any tax owed to Uncle Sam for the same income. If you don't have any net income in the United States, due to depreciation expense, then you have to carry forward the tax credit. Eventually, you may be able to use it. Note, though, that if you're an American holding foreign property in your own name, that's really the only difference for your U.S. tax-reporting requirements.

Taxes are the first potential ongoing management concern for any piece of property you own overseas. The other is property and rental management if you intend to rent the place out when you're not using it. I offer guidelines for this in Chapter 6.

What Every Overseas Property Buyer Needs to Know about Moving Money around the World

Key to buying a piece of real estate in another country is getting the cash required to close the sale where it needs to be when it needs to be there. In fact, as a would-be overseas property owner, you potentially face four international money management requirements. First, when you buy; second, if you renovate; third, if you rent your place out when you're not using it; and fourth, if and when you sell.

The most important thing to understand before wiring money to another country is whether that country imposes any currency restrictions. Most don't, but some do, as we've discussed. If the country where you intend to buy real estate does, you want to know what the restrictions are before you agree to any purchase there. This is something to discuss and clarify with your local attorney. Colombia, for example, requires that any incoming funds be registered with the country's central bank. If the funds are for living expenses, for example, then you complete one form (Form 4). If the funds are for investment, then you complete a different form (Form 5), indicating what type of investment you're making. If you complete the incorrect form or fail to file one at all, you will have a difficult time repatriating your capital and any associated profits. Complete and file all the paperwork correctly, and you should have no problem taking your money back out of the country if and when you decide you'd like to.

Brazil imposes similar rules. In this case, though, friends who've bought in this country report that, even if all the paperwork has been processed as called for, it still can be difficult to get your money out. Argentina recently put such strict controls in place that getting any hard currency out of that country is all but impossible. The Argentine currency controls likely will be eased in time, but right now they are a serious deterrent.

Escrow doesn't exist in most of the world. This is because title companies don't exist in most of the world, and it's usually title companies that handle escrow. Typically, therefore, when sending money for the purchase of real estate in another country, you'll be sending your funds to your *notaire* or your attorney, who, depending on the country, may have a client escrow account. This can work if you trust your attorney with that much money (even an honest guy can be tempted to "retire" early if enough money is made available to him). Another option would be to send the funds to your own bank account in the country and have your bank issue a certified check to hand over to the seller at closing. Or, if you can get the seller to agree, you could use a U.S. escrow company. However, most sellers in most of the world won't understand what escrow is, and, if they do, they won't like the idea of the funds for the closing sitting in another country. In the case of Argentina, the currency house you're using for the transaction effectively acts as the escrow company.

Regardless of the final solution, you'll be wiring the funds required. Some online banking systems allow you to initiate a wire from your account online, but if you're new to international wires, I'd recommend going into your bank branch to request the wire and fill out the paperwork in person. The timing is important, as you'll need to initiate the wire in time to allow the funds to arrive well in advance of the closing date. Depending on the routing, a wire from a U.S. bank to a Latin American bank can arrive the same day or it can take up to a week. Wires to Europe typically take three to five business days. Much can depend on the correspondent bank. With one, the wire might arrive the same day; with another, it could take up to five days. Much, too, depends on the receiving bank. Some banks post incoming wires to clients' account within 24 hours; others hold the money in limbo for a few days. There's nothing you can do about this except be informed and prepared.

To send a wire, you'll need instructions from the receiving bank, whether it's your own bank or that of your attorney. Financial institutions in the United States use mostly ABA numbers for in-country transfers and SWIFT numbers for incoming international wires. The IBAN system, used mostly in Europe, is more efficient, as the coding for an IBAN number includes both your bank and your account information, mitigating the risk of misrouting.

The wire instructions may include information about the recipient bank's correspondent bank or intermediary bank. Much of the time this isn't necessary, though, as banks can access this information on their own. Most banks work with more than one intermediary bank, so don't be alarmed if the wire instructions you're provided include options or a chain of banks.

Increasingly, any sending bank is going to ask for full address details for the recipient bank and the owner of the recipient bank account. The sending bank may require phone numbers for both, as well. It's best to ask your bank what details it requires for an international wire before making a transfer request.

If you're wiring the funds to your attorney's client account, notify your attorney when you request the wire. Provide the attorney with details of the sending bank and the amount of the wire, so that he's able to confirm receipt with his bank and to make sure the funds are properly credited to you.

Note that if you purchase preconstruction, you'll have a series of money management requirements. You'll make a down payment when you sign the purchase agreement, and then you'll make staged payments to the developer throughout the construction process, with one final payment due at closing. In the case of a preconstruction purchase from a developer, you can opt to wire funds directly to the developer. This works as long as the country imposes no currency or flow-of-funds restrictions (again, most countries where you'd be interested in buying don't), and it simplifies things, removing one layer of risk. In the case of Colombia or Brazil, however, or any other country that does impose currency controls, the best option is typically to wire funds into your account or your attorney's account so that you can be certain the money is properly registered. Then arrange a transfer from your account or your attorney's account to that of the developer.

If you purchase a place that requires renovation work, you'll have additional money management requirements. You'll need to get money into the country as required to cover the associated costs. In this case, you'll have to have your own local bank account to which to wire funds and from which to pay your contractor, electrician, plumber, carpenter, and so on.

Sometimes It Makes Sense to "Buy Ahead"

If you're intending to send a large amount of funds of one currency (say U.S. dollars) to a country where the currency is something else, you have an exchange issue that could work in your favor, or not. I'll preface my recommendations in this context by reminding you that you shouldn't try to time currency movements. You can't. Nobody can. You can, though, if you deem it prudent, eliminate future currency risk by locking in a current rate of exchange. You can also make sure that you get the best possible rate of exchange at the time you transfer your funds. You accomplish both of these things by running the money you intend to transfer through a foreign exchange house.

Say you want to buy an apartment in Paris or a farmhouse in Tuscany. You'll need euro. Wire the money for the purchase from your U.S. bank account directly to Europe (either to an account you hold there or to your attorney or *notaire*'s account), and in most cases, your U.S. bank will exchange your U.S. dollars into euro before making the transfer. The more money you send, the better the exchange rate the bank will give you, but generally speaking, the rate of exchange used won't be the best possible or even a good one. For small wires, it may not be worth the trouble, but if you're sending a sizable amount, you could benefit significantly from the better rate of exchange available from a foreign exchange company. The difference between the conversion rate used by your bank and the one used by a foreign exchange house could mean the difference of a few hundred or even a few thousand dollars.

In addition, if you're concerned about which way a currency is moving versus the U.S. dollar, you can remove any future exchange risk by buying that currency ahead of time. Returning to our Italian farmhouse example, say you're planning to buy next summer. Your budget is $200,000. You could exchange $200,000 now for euro, with the help of an exchange company, and then sit on those euro until time for closing. This could work to your advantage or against you, but it could also allow you to sleep better at night between now and whenever you finally close on your euro purchase.

HiFX (www.hifx.co.uk) is one exchange house that I've worked with in the past. HiFX's entire business is foreign exchange. They are trading and moving currencies back and forth, one to another, all day every day, and therefore, can give you a better exchange rate than your bank. Working with a group like HiFX requires setting up an account, which is similar to opening a bank account. That accomplished, you have access to their better rates. This strategy can make particularly good sense if you know you'll be sending multiple wires for a renovation, staged preconstruction payments, or mortgage payments.

How and Why to Open a Local Bank Account

As I've mentioned, sometimes you'll have the need to receive funds in another country directly. Maybe you'll want to wire your own funds from the United States to yourself in a place where you're renovating a house you've bought. If you invest in a piece of property that you rent out, you'll need to be able to take receipt of the rent each month. In addition, as a property owner anywhere in the world, you'll have local expenses—property taxes, perhaps; other taxes; building fees; and electric, gas, phone, cable, and Internet bills. I've known people who have tried to manage these things without benefit of a local bank account, but it's not easy and I'd say not worth it. The only reason to try to accomplish these things without a local bank account would be because you're unable to open a local bank account for some reason.

This isn't out of the question, as unfortunately, it's getting harder all the time for an American to open a bank account in many parts of the world. It can be difficult, but it should almost never be impossible if you have a valid reason for wanting the account. Owning property in the country is a valid reason.

To open a bank account in another country, you'll need your passport, a second ID (your driver's license works), and a reference letter from at least one bank back home. You may also be asked for a reference letter from your attorney or your accountant. This is another reason to use a local attorney for your real estate transaction, as he'll be able to provide a banking letter if you need one.

Be sure to ask about the bank's online access. You'll want to be able to check balances, move money, and, if possible, pay bills online. Most banks in most of the world offer online banking access these days. However, the level of service likely won't be what you are used to back home, and it may not be in English.

If you're intending to rent your place out, then I suggest opening a savings account as well as a checking account. This way, you can use the checking account as an operating account and move excess funds, as they accumulate, into the savings account. Don't keep a lot of money in your overseas checking account if you can help it. Forged checks and cloned ATM cards are not uncommon in some countries, and most banks in most of the world aren't going to make good if money is stolen from your account in either of these ways.

In that case, you may be wondering, wouldn't it be prudent to transfer excess funds, as they accumulate, from the foreign checking account to a U.S. savings or investment account? Typically, no. One big reason to be buying real estate overseas is for diversification, including currency diversification. If you transfer all the rental revenues that you earn from your rental property in another country to U.S. dollars in a U.S. bank account, you're interfering with your diversification agenda. One reason I bought an apartment in Medellín recently was to diversify into Colombia, including the economy and the currency. I want any rental revenues earned there to stay there, accumulating in Colombian pesos.

When you accumulate enough funds in your overseas savings account to warrant it, you could consider other options for holding cash in that country.

You could open a local CD, invest in the local stock market, use the money as the down payment on a next real estate purchase, or view the cash as a fund to cover personal expenses whenever you're in the country. Say you spend six months in France each year and rent your apartment out the rest of the year. You should (given that all things go according to plan and after all expenses and bills have been covered) end up with extra euro in your French bank account. You could use those euro to cover living expenses when you're in residence yourself, reducing your exchange rate risk. Rather than having to convert dollars to euro for every visit, you'll have cash earned as euro to spend as euro.

When You Exit

What about when you decide to sell? Then the proceeds from the sale can be deposited into your local bank account. If the country where you're selling imposes currency restrictions, you will definitely want to have the funds put into your local account. Then you'll file the proper paperwork allowing you to wire the funds out of the country if that's your plan. Before you take that lump sum and return it to U.S. dollars and U.S. shores, consider your options. Remember that one big objective of the original property purchase was diversification. Bringing the proceeds from the sale of that piece of property back into the United States undermines that agenda.

If you're intending to buy something new in the same country, your decision is easy. Leave the money where it is until you're ready for your next purchase. If you're thinking of buying in another country, again I'd suggest leaving the money where it is while you finalize your plans (unless the interim period extends indefinitely; in that case, you may want to find a better use for the sale proceeds in the meantime).

As an American, you'll have the same tax implications when you sell your overseas property as you would when selling a piece of property in the United States. If it's been your primary residence per the IRS regulations, you can exempt gains from U.S. tax up to the current limits (right now that's $250,000 for a single taxpayer and $500,000 for a couple).

If you purchase rental property overseas, you'll then be required to file a Schedule E with your U.S. returns. You'll also be able to recognize associated depreciation of the asset for U.S. tax purposes. When you sell an overseas rental property, you'll be liable for depreciation recapture taxes along with any capital gains tax on the amount above your original basis.

You'll also likely have some tax obligation in the country where the property is located, although not all countries charge capital gains taxes on real estate (Croatia, New Zealand, and Argentina, for example, do not). Most countries that tax capital gains from the sale of real estate do so at particular rates separate from other capital gains rates. A few countries tax gains on the sale of real estate as ordinary income, meaning that the tax rate is determined by the standard marginal tax bands. Don't worry about paying taxes twice on your gains. If your gain is taxable in both the country where the property is located and the United States, then you'll be able to take a tax credit on the U.S. side, limiting your total tax to the maximum due in either country. For example, if you pay 10 percent tax in the country where the property is located, then you'll pay another 5 percent (for 2012) in the United States. If you pay 30 percent tax in the country where the property is located, then you'll owe nothing in the United States.

Note that if the property is held by a corporation, it is customary for the shares of the company to be sold (instead of the property itself), thus eliminating local transfer tax.

One tax benefit available to U.S. investors in property overseas is the 1031 like-kind exchange. Briefly, this is a tax loophole that allows a real estate investor to defer tax on gains by following specific rules allowing him or her to reinvest the proceeds from the sale of one property into the purchase of another. Most U.S. investors take advantage of this strategy when selling one piece of U.S. investment property to buy another.

This loophole works for U.S. taxpayers when they sell foreign property as well, but only when the funds are invested in other foreign property. You have to avoid tax on the gains by transferring the proceeds from one piece of property to the purchase of another, but it must be U.S. property for U.S. property or foreign for foreign.

Before using this tax rule with real estate overseas, be sure that it makes sense. If you're paying a capital gains tax in the foreign country anyway, then the advantage of deferring your U.S. tax through a 1031 like-kind exchange probably isn't as great as taking the credit for the taxes paid in the other country. If you were, say, selling a piece of investment property in New Zealand, however, with the intention of using those proceeds to purchase another piece of investment property in Colombia, then the like-kind exchange could be a great benefit. You wouldn't be paying capital gains tax in New Zealand (as it doesn't charge any), so deferring U.S. tax is the right choice.

VI

Where Not to Buy

Markets Perhaps Better Avoided

tarting in the early 1980s, Costa Rica began working aggressively to solicit American retirees, even hiring a Madison Avenue ad agency to brand the country as the "world's top overseas retirement haven." The copywriters did their job. Ask any American about places to retire abroad, and she or he will likely mention Costa Rica. It wasn't a tough sell. Costa Rica is blessed with loads of natural beauty and two coastlines, including one on the Pacific that resembles the best of the southern California coast. Plus, back then, both life and real estate in Costa Rica were cheap. The country instituted a *pensionado* program of discounts and tax savings for foreign retirees to clinch the deal.

Given the costs, the special benefits, and the beauty of the landscapes all around, retirees didn't mind putting up with San José, which is dirty and crowded and can be unsafe. They were even happy to overlook the country's broken-down infrastructure. What did it matter if the road was unpaved and rutted? Your dream home at the end of it—with the crashing Pacific just beyond your front door—was a bargain.

That was 30 years ago. Costa Rica is a different place today. San José is as unappealing as ever and less safe. The rest of the country is still beautiful but not altogether safe either. Crime has become a big concern for both travelers and foreign retirees. Plus, in 1992, after working so hard the previous decade to woo American and European retirees, Costa Rica seemed to change its mind. The Costa Ricans didn't eliminate their *pensionado* program, but they did eliminate most of the tax breaks it had promised as part of a deficit-reduction austerity package, and they didn't grandfather existing *pensionados*. So those who'd chosen Costa Rica for the retiree benefits it offered were surprised and disappointed to find that those benefits no longer existed.

Through it all, the cost of living in this country increased steadily (Costa Rica has experienced high single-digit or low double-digit inflation, as high as 13.8 percent, every year for years) and the cost of real estate ballooned, but the infrastructure remained status quo—that is, broken down. The foreign retiree's home in Costa Rica was still at the end of a rutted dirt road (typically), but it was no longer a bargain. All countries in any part of the world make infrastructure promises they don't keep, but in Costa Rica it's the rule, not the exception. A new highway from San José to the Pacific coast was discussed for more than two decades before it was begun. Finally, before it was begun, it was drawn on some maps. It must exist by now, mapmakers must have thought, and so they began including it. (This road has since been built, by the way.) *A.M. Costa Rica* reported recently, the country's "deplorable road and bridge conditions have created a recipe for disaster. Roads in Costa Rica," the article continued, "are much the same as they were 30 years ago. However, during that time, the population has doubled and so has the number of cars on the roadways. Obsolete traffic circles are still used in San José, and a minor traffic accident can cause jams of up to five hours. For a country that wants to become part of the developed world, Costa Rica has to address governmental institutions plagued with problems and delays. The problem, of course, is that the country is broke."

Then came 2008, and the foreign property buyers who'd made this market all but disappeared. I know developers in Costa Rica who haven't made a sale since, and I've heard of many bargain-priced distress offerings. Still, I receive e-mails regularly from developers in this country that go like this: "This is a fast-moving market right now. Prices are climbing again. You can bank on continued appreciation. Your readers will want to get in quickly, because there are only so many lots available . . ."

Should you think about buying real estate in Costa Rica in this market? Although it remains perhaps the world's most recognized overseas property investment and retirement haven, I don't recommend it for the reasons I've explained. That said, you could have other reasons to consider owning here. When a friend was looking to relocate his family from the United States to Central America several years ago, he shopped around, and he chose Costa Rica over all the options in this part of the world for two good reasons. First, the weather in the hills surrounding San José is considerably more pleasant than the weather in Panama City (the other location he considered seriously), as it is cooler and less humid. Second, the international schooling options in San José are perhaps the best in the region. Panama City offers top choices, too, but David was most impressed by the international standard, English-language options that Costa Rica offered for educating his two school-aged children. In other words, David chose Costa Rica for lifestyle, rather than investment reasons. Perhaps you would too, given the chance, and nobody could argue with that.

I highlight Costa Rica in this way not to pick on it but to make the point that, unless you're considering buying real estate purely for personal and lifestyle reasons, not everywhere in the world makes sense as a place to diversify in this way.

Bulgaria was seen as the "next Spain" by British buyers in the run-up to this country's entry into the European Union in 2007. When Spanish property prices rose beyond the reach of some would-be British retirees and sun seekers, many swarmed to Bulgaria instead, where prices for preconstruction apartment units were as low as 20,000 pounds (and, yes, they were priced in pounds sterling, taking the targeted buyer's perspective). Bulgaria's weather can't compete with Spain's, but this fact seemed lost on British buyers at the time.

Then came 2008. Bulgaria's real estate market collapsed. Prices fell as much as 40 percent from their peaks, and all the British sun worshippers and retirees disappeared overnight. The Brits had been buying because developers were marketing to them. Bulgarian real estate booths were prominent at UK overseas property shows. Agents sold well thanks to the low prices and preconstruction terms. On a unit priced at 20,000 pounds, the down payment was as little as 2,000 pounds. This didn't even cover the commissions developers were paying. I know this because Bulgarian developers approached me to ask about participating in my conferences. They were offering commissions as high as 20 percent. Imagine the apartment that you were buying in Bulgaria when you were paying 20,000 and only 16,000 pounds were going in to the property. It costs more than that to furnish an apartment in most of the world.

Once the Brits left the market in 2008, the Russians stepped in to fill the gap. Russians are among today's biggest foreign buyers throughout Europe. In Bulgaria, they shopped for small one-bedroom apartments in the range of 30,000 euro to use as part-time vacation homes and to rent out when they weren't using them. This demand led to further overbuilding. The result is that, although you can buy cheap in Bulgaria, you have better options elsewhere for both living and investing.

Where else might you proceed with caution? Asia. It's not that you shouldn't invest in real estate in that part of the world, full stop. I have colleagues who have done well investing in Thailand, Cambodia, the Philippines, Malaysia, and China. The problem generally is that foreigners can't own property in most Asian countries, at least not in the way we Westerners think about property ownership. In some countries, foreign ownership is outright forbidden. In others you can't take freehold title, but you can own via leasehold (or a similar concept).

Of the countries where we foreigners can't own at all, Cambodia is interesting. Friends have made good profits here. One is married to a Cambodian and living in the country. Title for the property he's purchased has been put into his wife's name. Another friend has Cambodian friends he trusts enough to have them hold title (paying them something for the trouble). The risks should be obvious in both cases.

Thailand and the Philippines allow foreigners to own up to 50 percent of the units in any condo building. I guess they figure that if foreigners own less than a controlling interest in the construction, they can't control the land beneath the building. The option in these countries is to own property leasehold. Leasehold means that you don't have automatic rights to the land in perpetuity. Typically, your initial lease is for a given period of time, which can then be renewed at least once for an additional period. If you aren't concerned about legacy planning, this type of ownership could be fine. Most leases renew out long after you'd be around to worry about it.

Malaysia imposes a minimum purchase requirement for foreigners, as well as land ownership restrictions. The minimum buy for foreigners is meant to keep them from bidding up affordable housing for locals. Nevertheless, Kuala Lumpur can be an interesting market both for personal use and for rental investment.

The rules in Vietnam are even more restrictive. No one, not even the Vietnamese, can own land. It's all owned by the government. Foreigners who live in the country can buy a house with the right to use the land (similar to leasehold, but not quite the same thing). They can also hold title to a condo in certain approved developments with 50-year leases on the land. Renewal of the lease isn't guaranteed and being non-Vietnamese requires a dangerous shell game with companies that I don't recommend.

In Thailand and the Philippines, too, foreigners have to engage in workarounds using local corporations to own real estate, in these cases obtaining fee simple title. These workarounds are risky and also illegal. Further, corporations in Thailand and the Philippines (with certain exceptions that won't help with real estate) can't be majority-owned by foreigners. Therefore, your corporation may hold freehold title to the property you buy, but you must trust locals who must hold your shares and attorneys who must structure these deals. You're better off with leasehold.

Ownership restrictions and requirements are one obstacle. In addition, most Asian markets have other quirks that make them complicated and risky places to invest. Further, these aren't places to consider for full-time retirement, as it's not possible (except in Malaysia and the Philippines) to obtain full-time legal residency.

Appendix A
Market Data

Two notes about the country data that follow: First, it's not easy to compile this kind of data reliably. Search for it on the Internet, and you'll find conflicting facts and figures in many cases. This is because information like this can be unreliable on the Internet. It's also because these particulars change all the time. As of this writing, Ireland is preparing to impose a property tax, although none has existed in this country for decades; Spain is imposing a temporary property "surcharge" that amounts to a property tax; and Panama's long-standing property tax exemption allowance has finally, after many renewals, lapsed. This leads to my second point, which is that the following information is correct as I write, based not on Internet research but my own personal experience and that of colleagues I trust. It may not, however, be complete or completely accurate when you proceed with a purchase in one of these countries. Use the following data, therefore, as a guide. These are the details that you should confirm with your local attorney in advance of signing any contract.

Argentina

Language: Spanish

Currency: Argentine peso

Form of Government: federal representative presidential republic

Inflation Rate: 22 percent (official; the actual rate is likely higher)

Foreign Investment Restrictions: Areas near national borders require approval from the government. Foreigners cannot own more than 1,000 hectares of rural land.

Real Estate Agent Fees: 3 to 4 percent paid by the buyer and 3 to 4 percent paid by the seller

Attorney Fees: not required

Notary (escribano) Fees: 1 to 2 percent paid by the buyer

Registration Fees: 42 pesos

Transfer Tax/Stamp Duty: 1.5 percent paid by the seller (does not apply if seller buys another home within 12 months) and 2.5 to 4 percent levied by the province that can be split between the buyer and the seller

Withholding Tax: none

Capital Gains Tax: none

Rental Income Tax: 21 percent

Property Tax: 0 percent in Buenos Aires, 1.25 percent elsewhere in the country

Bank Financing Available: no

Getting Started Resource: Paul Reynolds, Reynolds Propriedades, www .homes.com.ar, paul@realestate.com.ar

Belize

Language: English

Currency: Belize dollar, pegged 2 to 1 to the U.S. dollar

Form of Government: unitary parliamentary constitutional monarchy

Inflation Rate: 2 percent

Foreign Investment Restrictions: none

Real Estate Agent Fees: 7 percent for residential property, 10 percent for raw land, usually paid by the seller but can be split with the buyer

Attorney Fees: optional and negotiable, typically 1 to 3 percent

Notary Fees: none

Registration Fees: around BZ$15

Transfer Tax/Stamp Duty: 5 percent paid by the buyer; first BZ$20,000 is exempt

Withholding Tax: none

Capital Gains Tax: none

Rental Income Tax: 3 percent

Property Tax: 1 to 1.5 percent of the value of the undeveloped land

Bank Financing Available: yes

    Maximum loan-to-value ratio: 60 percent

    Maximum term: 15 years

    Life insurance required: no

Maximum age for a mortgage: none

Interest rate: 12 to 14 percent

Debt-to-income ratio maximum: varies by lender

Residency necessary to borrow: no

Getting Started Resource: Macarena Rose, Rain Forest Realty, www.rain forestrealty.net, macarenarose@gmail.com

Brazil

Language: Portuguese

Currency: real

Form of Government: federal presidential constitutional republic

Inflation Rate: 7 percent

Foreign Investment Restrictions: Total agricultural land owned by foreigners in any given state may not exceed 2 percent of total agricultural land in the state.

Real Estate Agent Fees: 5 to 6 percent paid by the seller

Attorney Fees: 0.5 to 2 percent paid by the buyer

Notary Fees: 2 to 3 percent

Registration Fees: included in the notary fee and transfer tax

Transfer Tax/Stamp Duty: 2 to 6 percent (3 percent average) depending on the municipality

Withholding Tax: none

Capital Gains Tax: 15 percent

Rental Income Tax: 15 percent

Property Tax: 0.3 to 1 percent on urban properties depending on the municipality; 0.003 to 20 percent on rural property depending on the location and land use

Bank Financing Available: no

Getting Started Resource: Paulo Peixoto, www.peixotoadvocacia.com, paulopeixoto@peixotoadvocacia.com

Chile

Language: Spanish

Currency: Chilean peso

Form of Government: unitary presidential republic

Inflation Rate: 3 percent

Foreign Investment Restrictions: none

Real Estate Agent Fees: 2 percent paid by the buyer and 2 percent paid by the seller

Attorney Fees: 1 to 2.5 percent paid by the buyer

Notary Fees: 0.1 percent with a maximum charge of 128,000 pesos paid by the buyer

Registration Fees: 13,500 pesos

Transfer Tax/Stamp Duty: 0.2 to 0.3 percent with a maximum charge of 260,000 pesos

Withholding Tax: none

Capital Gains Tax: 17 percent

Rental Income Tax: 17 percent

Property Tax: 1.4 percent on urban property, 1 percent on rural property

Bank Financing Available: no

Getting Started Resource: Micheal Stronach, www.sj.cl/, stronach@sj.cl

Colombia

Language: Spanish

Currency: Colombian peso

Form of Government: unitary presidential constitutional republic

Inflation Rate: 3.4 percent

Foreign Investment Restrictions: none

Real Estate Agent Fees: 3 percent paid by the seller and 3 percent paid by the buyer

Attorney Fees: negotiable, around 0.5 percent paid by the buyer

Notary Fees: 0.27 to 0.3 percent split between the buyer and the seller

Registration Fees: 1 percent registration tax, 0.05 percent registration fee, both paid by the buyer

Transfer Tax/Stamp Duty: 0.15 percent paid by the seller and 0.15 percent paid by the buyer

Withholding Tax: 1 percent paid by the seller

Capital Gains Tax: 33 percent

Rental Income Tax: 19 to 33 percent, 33 percent flat tax for nonresidents

Property Tax: 0.01 to 1.6 percent depending on the municipality

Bank Financing Available: no

Getting Started Resource: Juan Dario Gutierrez, Gutierrez Marquez Asesores S.A., www.gutierrezmarquez.com, juandgutierrez@gutierrez marquez.com

Croatia

Language: Croatian

Currency: kuna

Form of Government: unitary parliamentary constitutional republic

Inflation Rate: 2 percent

Foreign Investment Restrictions: Requires consent from the Ministry of Foreign Affairs, which is dependent on reciprocity with foreign national's home country (that is, whether Croatians can purchase real estate in that country). Foreigners may not purchase agricultural or forestry land; these restrictions can be circumvented by setting up a Croatian corporation to purchase the property on your behalf.

Real Estate Agent Fees: 3 to 6 percent split between the buyer and the seller

Attorney Fees: 1 to 1.5 percent paid by the buyer

Notary Fees: 47 kuna paid by the buyer

Registration Fees: 200 kuna paid by the buyer

Transfer Tax/Stamp Duty: 5 percent paid by the buyer. Note: The sale of newly built property may be subject to a 25 percent value added tax in addition to the 5 percent transfer tax on the land value.

Withholding Tax: 25 percent

Capital Gains Tax: 25 percent. Note: Seller can avoid capital gains tax if the property sold was (1) the owner's principal residence, (2) held more than three years, or (3) sold to a spouse or immediate family member.

Rental Income Tax: 15 percent

Property Tax: none

Bank Financing Available: no

Getting Started Resource: Markovic & Pliso, markovic-pliso@zg.tel.hr

Dominican Republic

Language: Spanish

Currency: Dominican Republic peso

Form of Government: representative democracy

Inflation Rate: 9 percent

Foreign Investment Restrictions: none

Real Estate Agent Fees: 5 to 10 percent, negotiable, paid by the seller

Attorney Fees: 1 percent paid by the buyer

Notary Fees: included with attorney fees

Registration Fees: 2 percent paid by the buyer

Transfer Tax/Stamp Duty: 3 percent paid by the buyer plus a document stamp tax of 232 pesos on the first 20,000 pesos of the property value and 13 pesos for every 1,000 pesos of value thereafter

Withholding Tax: none

Capital Gains Tax: 25 percent for nonresidents and 0 percent for sale value up to 330,301 pesos, 15 percent for 330,301.01 to 495,450 pesos, 20 percent for 495,450.01 to 688,125 pesos, 25 percent over 688,125.01 pesos for residents

Rental Income Tax: 25 percent for nonresidents and 0 percent for sale value up to 330,301 pesos, 15 percent for 330,301.01 to 495,450 pesos, 20 percent for 495,450.01 to 688,125 pesos, 25 percent over 688,125.01 pesos for residents

Property Tax: 1 percent of value exceeding 6 million pesos

Bank Financing Available: yes

  Maximum loan-to-value ratio: 80 percent

  Maximum term: 20 years

  Life insurance required: by some banks

  Maximum age for a mortgage: 65 years

  Interest rate: 9.5 to 10.95 percent

  Debt-to-income ratio maximum: 70 percent

  Residency necessary to borrow: no

Getting Started Resource: Aaron, Suero & Pedersini, dlawyers@codetel .net.do

Ecuador

Language: Spanish

Currency: U.S. dollar

Form of Government: unitary presidential constitutional republic

Inflation Rate: 5 percent

Foreign Investment Restrictions: Foreigners may not own property within 50 kilometers of the national borders.

Real Estate Agent Fees: 3 to 4 percent paid by the seller

Attorney Fees: $700 to $850 paid by the buyer

Notary Fees: 0.3 percent paid by the buyer

Registration Fees: $118 + 0.5 percent paid by the buyer

Transfer Tax/Stamp Duty: 1 percent paid by the buyer

Withholding Tax: none

Capital Gains Tax: 0.5 percent on the difference between the purchase and sale price

Rental Income Tax: 25 percent

Property Tax: 0.025 to 0.5 percent

Bank Financing Available: no

Getting Started Resource: Bruce Horowitz, www.pazhorowitz.com, bhorowitz@pazhorowitz.com

Important note for Ecuador: Although taxes and fees may seem high, they are based on the municipal (or assessed) value, rather than the sale price. Municipal values are typically between 30 percent and 60 percent of the sale price. You can expect closing costs in Ecuador to be around 2 percent of the sale price.

France

Language: French

Currency: euro

Form of Government: unitary semipresidential constitutional republic

Inflation Rate: 2.3 percent

Foreign Investment Restrictions: none

Real Estate Agent Fees: 5 to 10 percent usually paid by the buyer but can be split with the seller

Attorney Fees: a *notaire* (notary) handles property transactions in France

Notary (notaire) Fees: about 1 percent

Registration Fees: included with stamp duty

Transfer Tax/Stamp Duty: 5.09 percent

Withholding Tax: none

Capital Gains Tax: 34.5 percent

Rental Income Tax: 35.5 percent

Property Tax: Two property taxes are imposed (*taxe de habitation* and *taxe fonciere*) and vary according to local authorities; total is about 0.2 percent in Paris.

Bank Financing Available: yes

Maximum loan-to-value ratio: 85 percent

Maximum term: 15 to 30 years depending on the bank

Life insurance required: yes

Maximum age for a mortgage: 80

Variable interest rates from: 2.70 percent

Fixed interest rates from: 3.25 percent

Debt-to-income ratio maximum: 50 percent

Residency necessary to borrow: no

Getting Started Resource: Stephan Adler, *notaire* in Paris, scp.bonnart@paris.notaires.fr

Ireland

Language: English

Currency: euro

Form of Government: parliamentary constitutional republic

Inflation Rate: 2.6 percent

Foreign Investment Restrictions: none

Real Estate Agent Fees: 1 to 3 percent paid by the buyer and 1 to 3 percent paid by the seller

Attorney Fees: usually 1 percent

Notary Fees: none

Registration Fees: 125 to 625 euro

Transfer Tax/Stamp Duty: 1 percent on first 1 million euro of value, 2 percent on the excess

Withholding Tax: 15 percent

Capital Gains Tax: 30 percent

Rental Income Tax: 20 percent

Property Tax: 100 euro; note that a value-based property tax is in the works

Bank Financing Available: yes

Maximum loan-to-value ratio: 80 percent for nonresidents, 85 percent for residents

Maximum term: 35 years with Allied Irish Banks (AIB)
Life insurance required: yes
Maximum age for a mortgage: 70
Fixed interest rate: 5.90 percent
Variable interest rate: 3.63 percent
Debt-to-income ratio maximum: varies by lender
Residency necessary to borrow: no
Getting Started Resource: Therese Rochford, Whitney Moore Solicitors, http://www.whitneymoore.ie

Italy

Language: Italian
Currency: euro
Form of Government: unitary parliamentary constitutional republic
Inflation Rate: 2.9 percent
Foreign Investment Restrictions: none
Real Estate Agent Fees: between 4 percent and 6 percent split between the buyer and seller
Attorney Fees: 1 to 2.50 percent paid by the buyer
Notary Fees: 1 to 2 percent + 20 percent value added tax paid by the buyer
Registration Fees: 3 to 7 percent paid by the buyer
Transfer Tax/Stamp Duty: The amount, 3 to 10 percent, depends on whether you are buying urban or rural property and how you intend to use the property.
Withholding Tax: 20 percent
Capital Gains Tax: 0 percent on property held for more than five years; 5 to 30 percent on property held for less than five years depending on the type and location of property
Rental Income Tax: 19 to 46 percent depending on the value of the property
Property Tax: vary according to the local authority, from 0.4 percent to 0.7 percent
Bank Financing Available: yes
Maximum loan-to-value ratio: 80 percent
Maximum term: 30 years
Life insurance required: not usually

Maximum age for a mortgage: 85

Variable interest rate: from 4.60 percent

Fixed interest rate: from 4.70 percent

Debt-to-income ratio maximum: 35 percent

Residency necessary to borrow: no

Getting Started Resource: Nikki DiGirolamo, www.housearounditaly.com, nikki@housearounditaly.com

Malaysia

Language: Malay

Currency: ringgit

Form of Government: federal constitutional elective monarchy and federal parliamentary democracy

Inflation Rate: 3.2 percent

Foreign Property Restrictions: Foreigners can purchase only property with a minimum value of 250,000 ringgit and are allowed to purchase only up to two residential properties, specifically: two condominiums in buildings with no more than 50 percent foreign ownership OR one condominium and one of the following—(1) terrace or linked house above two stories (limited to 10 percent of the total number of units built of this type) or (2) land/bungalow or semidetached house (limited to 10 percent of units built of these types).

Real Estate Agent Fees: 2 to 3 percent paid by the seller

Attorney Fees: 0.4 to 1 percent paid by the buyer

Notary Fees: 152 ringgit

Registration Fees:

Stamping Fee: 10 ringgit per document

Adjudication Fee: 10 ringgit

Title Search Fee: 60 ringgit

Registration Fee: 100 ringgit

Transfer Tax/Stamp Duty: 1 to 3 percent on property transfers and 0.3 percent on share transaction documents, in both cases paid by the buyer

Withholding Tax: 15 percent for nonresidents, 10 percent for residents

Capital Gains Tax: 10 percent for property held less than two years by nonresidents, 5 percent for property held for less than five years

Rental Income Tax: 26 percent

Property Tax: 6 percent

Bank Financing Available: no

Getting Started Resource: Mike Soo, Malaysia My Second Home, mike soo18@gmail.com

Mexico

Language: Spanish

Currency: Mexican peso

Form of Government: federal presidential constitutional republic

Inflation Rate: 3.4 percent

Foreign Property Restrictions: To own within 50 kilometers of the coast or 100 kilometers of an international border, foreigners must purchase through a *fidecomiso*, a real estate bank trust specifically created to hold property.

Real Estate Agent Fees: 3 to 7 percent + 15 percent VAT paid for by the seller

Attorney Fees: 13,000 to 65,000 pesos depending on the complexity of the transaction and where the transaction is taking place

Notary Fees: 1.5 percent paid for by the buyer

Registration Fees: 0.02 to 1.82 percent depending on where the transaction is taking place, paid by the buyer

Transfer Tax/Stamp Duty: 2 to 5 percent depending on where the transaction is taking place

Withholding Tax: 25 percent

Capital Gains Tax: 25 percent for nonresidents, 30 percent for residents

Rental Income Tax: 25 percent

Property Tax: 0.06 to 1.3 percent depending on where the property is located

Bank Financing Available: yes

    Maximum loan-to-value ratio: 80 percent

    Maximum term: 30 years

    Is life insurance required? No

    Maximum age for a mortgage: 65

    Variable interest rate: from 3.65 percent

    Fixed interest rate: from 6.25 percent

Debt-to-income ratio maximum: 42 percent

Residency necessary to borrow: no

Getting Started Resource: Conita Raviela, Asesoria Inmobilaria in Puerto Vallarta, ai.asesoriainmobiliaria@gmail.com

New Zealand

Language: English

Currency: New Zealand dollar

Form of Government: unitary parliamentary constitutional monarchy

Inflation Rate: 4 percent

Foreign Property Restrictions: Foreigners cannot own "sensitive land" without prior government consent; a standard suburban house would not be classified as sensitive, but a farm, rural, or waterfront property could fall under this category.

Real Estate Agent Fees: 3.5 to 4 percent + 12.5 percent gross sales tax paid by the seller

Attorney Fees: NZ$600 to NZ$2,000

Notary Fees: none

Registration Fees: NZ$20 to NZ$50

Transfer Tax/Stamp Duty: none

Withholding Tax: none

Capital Gains Tax: none with some exceptions that apply to real estate professionals and developers

Rental Income Tax: progressive rates, 10.5 to 33 percent

Property Tax: none

Bank Financing Available: yes

Maximum loan-to-value ratio: 95 percent

Maximum term: 30 years

Life insurance required: no

Maximum age for a mortgage: 70

Variable interest rate: from 5.99 percent

Fixed interest rate: from 4.85 percent

Debt-to-income ratio maximum: case by case

Residency necessary to borrow: no

Getting Started Resource: Cuningham Taylor, www.ctlaw.co.nz, ct@ctlaw.co.nz

Nicaragua

Language: Spanish

Currency: cordoba, but note that real estate trades in U.S. dollars

Form of Government: unitary presidential constitutional republic

Inflation Rate: 8.1 percent

Foreign Property Restrictions: none

Real Estate Agent Fees: 3 to 6 percent for residential, 7 to 10 percent for development land, paid by the seller

Attorney Fees: 1 percent

Notary Fees: 1.5 to 2 percent

Registration Fees: 1 percent

Transfer Tax/Stamp Duty: 3 percent paid by the buyer, 1 percent paid by the seller

Withholding Tax: 20 percent

Capital Gains Tax: none

Rental Income Tax: 20 percent

Property Tax: 1 percent

Bank Financing Available: no

Getting Started Resource: Turalu Brady Murdock, tueymurdock@gmail.com

Panama

Language: Spanish

Currency: U.S. dollar

Form of Government: unitary presidential constitutional republic

Inflation Rate: 5.9 percent

Foreign Property Restrictions: Foreigners cannot own within 10 kilometers of the border or on certain islands.

Real Estate Agent Fees: 3 to 5 percent paid by the seller

Attorney Fees: 1 to 2 percent paid by the buyer

Notary Fees: 2 percent

Registration Fees: up to US$2,500 depending on the value of the property

Transfer Tax/Stamp Duty: 2 percent of either the updated registered value of the property or the sale price, whichever is higher, paid by the seller

Withholding Tax: 3 percent

Capital Gains Tax: 10 percent

Rental Income Tax: none for property in special "tourism zones"; 15 to 27 percent otherwise, depending on the amount of rental income earned

Property Tax: none for property built with a property tax exemption (in this case, confirm the number of years of exemption remaining); otherwise 2.10 percent

Bank Financing Available: yes

Maximum loan-to-value ratio: 90 percent

Maximum term: 10 to 15 years is typical; 30 years can be possible

Is life insurance required? yes

Maximum age for a mortgage: 70

Variable interest rate: from 3.65 percent

Fixed interest rate: from 6.25 percent

Debt-to-income ratio maximum: 42 percent

Residency necessary to borrow: no

Getting Started Resource: Rainelda Mata-Kelly, www.mata-kelly.com, rmk@mata-kelly.com

Philippines

Language: Filipino

Currency: Philippine peso

Form of Government: unitary presidential constitutional republic

Inflation Rate: 4.8 percent

Foreign Property Restrictions: Foreigners cannot own land but can own houses and condominium units or apartments in high-rise buildings as long as the foreign-owned proportion does not exceed 40 percent of overall building ownership; foreigners can lease land for up to 50 years with the possibility of a 25-year renewal.

Real Estate Agent Fees: 3 to 5 percent paid by the seller

Attorney Fees: 20,000 pesos or, in some cases, 5 to 10 percent of the property value, paid by the buyer

Notary Fees: 200 pesos per title or document

Registration Fees: 4,398 pesos + 90 pesos for every 20,000 pesos in excess of 1.7 million pesos of property value

Transfer Tax/Stamp Duty: 0.50 to 0.75 percent paid by the buyer

Withholding Tax: 20 percent

Capital Gains Tax: 6 percent of the gross sales price or current fair market value, whichever is greater; an individual also is subject to capital gains tax on sales of shares not traded on the stock exchange at a rate of 5 percent of the net gain up to 100,000 pesos and 10 percent on the excess

Rental Income Tax: 25 percent

Property Tax: up to 3 percent of the assessed value depending on where the property is located

Bank Financing Available: no

Getting Started Resource: Sison, Corillo Parone & Co, www.scp-ph.com, scp@edsamail.com.ph

Romania

Language: Romanian

Currency: Romanian leu (euro expected by 2015)

Form of Government: unitary semipresidential republic

Inflation Rate: 5.8 percent

Foreign Property Restrictions: Foreigners cannot own land.

Real Estate Agent Fees: 6 percent split between buyer and seller

Notary Fees: 0.5 percent to 2 percent paid by the buyer

Registration Fees: 1 percent

Transfer Tax/Stamp Duty: up to 3 percent depending on the value of the property

Withholding Tax: 16 percent

Capital Gains Tax: none

Rental Income Tax: 16 percent

Property Tax: 0.25 to 1.5 percent depending on the property's location and value

Bank Financing Available: yes

Maximum loan-to-value ratio: 75 percent

Maximum term: 25 years is typical, 35 years may be possible

Life insurance required: no

Maximum age for a mortgage: 65 to 70 depending on the bank

Fixed interest rate: 7.65 percent

Variable interest rate: 6.35 percent

Debt-to-income ratio maximum: case by case

Residency necessary to borrow: no

Getting Started Resource: Adrian Niculescu, KBC Real Estate, adrian
.niculescu@kbc.ro

Spain

Language: Spanish
Currency: euro
Form of Government: parliamentary constitutional monarchy
Inflation Rate: 3.1 percent
Foreign Property Restrictions: none
Real Estate Agent Fees: 2.5 to 3 percent paid by the seller, but note that
  some agents may try to charge more
Attorney Fees: 100 to 250 euro per hour or 1 to 1.5 percent of the purchase
  price; negotiable
Notary Fees: 0.5 to 1 percent
Registration Fees: capped at 1,900 euro paid by the buyer
Transfer Tax/Stamp Duty: 6 to 10 percent depending on the region and
  property value
Withholding Tax: 3 percent
Capital Gains Tax: 19 percent on the first 6,000 euro profit and 21 percent
  on the excess
Rental Income Tax: 24 percent
Property Tax: Spain is temporarily imposing an annual property "sur-
  charge" of 10 percent
Bank Financing Available: yes
  Maximum loan-to-value ratio: 70 percent for nonresidents; residents
    can borrow up to 80 percent
  Maximum term: 40 years
  Life insurance required: not always
  Maximum age for a mortgage: 65 to 70 depending on the bank
  Fixed interest rate: 5.8 percent
  Variable interest rate: 4.35 percent
  Debt-to-income ratio maximum: 30 to 50 percent depending on the
    bank
  Residency necessary to borrow: no
Getting Started Resource: Rodriguez Molnar & Asociados, www.m-rm
  .com, firm@rm-as.com

Uruguay

Language: Spanish

Currency: Uruguayan peso

Form of Government: unitary presidential constitutional republic

Inflation Rate: 8.1 percent

Foreign Property Restrictions: none

Real Estate Agent Fees: 3.66 percent paid by the buyer and 3.66 percent paid by the seller

Notary Fees: 3 percent

Registration Fees: 1 percent paid by the buyer

Transfer Tax/Stamp Duty: 4 percent split between buyer and seller

Withholding Tax: 7 percent

Capital Gains Tax: 12 percent

Rental Income Tax: 12 percent

Property Tax: 0.25 to 0.5 percent depending on the property value

Bank Financing Available: yes

    Maximum loan-to-value ratio: 70 percent

    Maximum term: 15 to 20 years depending on the bank

    Is life insurance required? yes

    Maximum age for a mortgage: 60

    Fixed interest rate: 6 percent

    Variable interest rate: 5 percent

    Debt-to-income ratio maximum: 30 percent

    Residency necessary to borrow: yes

Getting Started Resource: Juan Federico Fischer, Fischer & Schickendantz, www.fs.com.uy, jfischer@fs.com.uy

Appendix B
Due Diligence Checklist

1. *Access:* How close is the nearest airport? Do you have to make a connection after arriving in the country? For rural properties, is there year-round access to the area? Not all roads are accessible year-round in Nicaragua, for example, or in parts of other countries in this region. For city properties, what are the traffic patterns? How will they affect your lifestyle or your ability to rent the property?
2. *Security:* How will security be provided? Apartment buildings in Latin America generally have doormen 24/7. In most buildings in France, the front door to the building or the building's courtyard, as the case may be, is kept locked at all times. Access is via a code shared with building residents only. Many buildings in France also have a concierge (although a concierge is more for service than security). If you're buying into a private development anywhere, you should expect 24/7 security at the entrance. If you're buying a farmhouse in the country, will you need to hire someone to keep an eye on the place?
3. *Medical Care:* Where is the nearest medical care facility? How many minutes to get there by car in both the wet and the dry seasons?
4. *Title Insurance:* Is title insurance available for the property from a reputable title insurance company? Insurance is available in most Latin American countries from either Stewart or First American Title and in much of Europe as well. If a developer or real estate agent tries to steer you away from getting title insurance, you should probably walk away from the deal. Title insurance isn't necessary, but it should be an option.
5. *Construction:* If you're buying a lot in a development, is there a building requirement (that is, a specified period of time within which you must build on your lot)? A building requirement is both a pro and a con.

With a requirement, you could be forced to build before you want or can afford to. Without it, you could be buying into a development that never develops. If no one is forced to build, you can't be sure anyone ever will.

6. *Development Community:* If you're buying into a planned development community, what construction and design standards are in place? This can be one of the big benefits of choosing this option rather than buying a house or a lot off on your own. Zoning is almost nonexistent in Latin America, and unless covenants and building restrictions are put in place (as in a private community), you may not like what your neighbors decide to erect next door.

7. *Infrastructure:* This is important on both a general country and a specific property or development level. At the country level, how often does the electricity go out in the region where you'll be living? How reliable are the cable and Internet services? What is the condition of the roads? How is water provided to the town or city? What about wastewater? Ask these questions of everyone you meet in the area.

On an individual property or development level, does the developer, apartment building, or house have a generator for when electricity goes out? How about water storage in case of interruption to the normal water supply? What amenities are in place? Is the building or property well maintained? Is there enough water and water pressure? Is there hot water? What's the plan for waste disposal? Either the developer has installed these systems and covered the costs, or he hasn't. If he hasn't, who will? (Hint: You are.)

When buying into a planned development, buy what you see. Do not take for granted that further infrastructure will be installed and do not believe every infrastructure promise that a developer makes. If you see paved roads, then there are paved roads. If you see a clubhouse, then there's a clubhouse. I say again: Buy what you see. And make sure that the price reflects the current reality. Don't pay a premium for "planned infrastructure."

8. *Homeowners Association (HOA):* What are the fees or, in the case of a new development or a preconstruction building, the projected fees? If you're buying into a completed development, ask to look at the current financial statements. Has the HOA management created a reserve fund? Do the expenses match the level of visible amenities and maintenance? Are things being maintained, or do you see a lot of

deferred maintenance? You should worry about both unusually low fees and deferred maintenance, because they may result in surprise assessments down the road.

For a building or planned community not turned over to the owners' management group yet, has the developer estimated the fees to a level that should maintain the planned amenities? Although no one wants to pay more than necessary for HOA fees, you also don't want to be lured in by a low projected fee only to have them go up substantially once the developer turns over maintenance to the owners. The costs will be what they are. If projected HOA fees don't cover them, one of two things will result. The property will slowly deteriorate or owners will be required to meet regular capital calls beyond the HOA amounts.

9. *Construction:* How will you build (if that's your plan) from thousands of miles away? Who will oversee construction for you? How often will you be able to visit the site yourself? I'd recommend at least monthly. When budgeting a construction project, understand what's included in the cost. You want to see written specifications, such as specifics to verify that 220-V water heaters and air conditioners and hot water lines to all sinks and showers are included. In Latin America, it's common to provide cold water only to guest and maid bathrooms. Also, confirm whether the quote you have includes lights, fans, faucets, fixtures, and appliances. Assume nothing.

10. *Amenities:* What amenities exist in the development or apartment building? Included are pools, parks, golf, tennis, fitness, clubhouse, and so on. These all have value, but they also cost money to maintain. What amenities/services are in the neighborhood? If you're buying an apartment in a city, you should walk the few blocks around the apartment to see what is nearby. Shops, restaurants, parking, parks, and public transportation can add value for rental and resale.

11. *Track Record:* If you're buying from a developer (either a lot in a planned community or a preconstruction apartment in a building that hasn't yet been completed), is the development company financially sound? Does the company have a track record?

Acknowledgments

I could not have written this book without the help of my husband, Lief Simon. He's my number cruncher, tax advisor, currency converter, and spreadsheet guru. He's also been my partner in every overseas real estate investment I've made throughout my career.

With one exception—the accidental developer experience I found myself involved with a few years before I met Lief, on the south Pacific coast of Nicaragua. For that, I have Bill Bonner and Mark Ford to thank, and I do.

In these pages I share stories of the overseas real estate adventures of friends with personal experience living, buying, and selling in the countries I feature, especially Paul Terhorst, who gives brilliant insights into why Argentina is the lovable basket case it is, and Lee Harrison, Lucy Culpepper, Ann Kuffner, Wendy Justice, and Coley Hudgins.

Thank you, also, to Denis Foynes and David Saxton, for all their quick research and reliable fact checking. The fruits of their labor are featured in Appendix A.

Thank you to Richard Narramore, both for proposing and developing this project and for helping me to clarify and broaden my understanding of things I'd thought I'd understood for years. Thank you to Lydia Dimitriadis for so skillfully shepherding the project at John Wiley & Sons.

Finally, thank you to all the attorneys whose counsel I've come to rely on around the world, especially Morette Kinsella in Ireland, Stephane Adler and Jean Taquet in France, Rainelda Mata-Kelly in Panama, Juan Federico Fischer in Uruguay, and Juan Dario Gutierrez in Colombia. Thank you for your continued support, your sound advice, your cool heads, your good company, and your valued friendship.

Index